FRANK E. GREENE JR.

ISBN: 979-8-89216-028-5 (Paperback)

BookmarcAlliance
California, USA
www.bookmarcalliance.com

Dedicated to my wife MARQUANEES

_____Colored People, the book. As review by severals critics. "This book has the potential; Telling another side of a story. Many history books fail to reveal."

_____"Colored People gaved me a whole new insight on how black folkes have struggle. Since they were brought to America"

A fellow writer.

_____I found this book, Colored Peoples. Telling the naked truths. During an era in history. When whites segregation its's rule." Another observer's wrote.

_____"Colored People, the story journey through a period. Where Negros and experience a holocaust of discrimination under JIM – CROW – LAWS." Another crite wrote

_____Although some of the language contents, is X-RATED. The story is well written. I believe millions of reader's will become awoken after reading this book."

Still another crite

FOREWORD

_____Who in their right mind, would write such a powerful story. About the lifes of Colored People. Unless he, himself have experience some of the same!

I, first met Timothy, some time ago. Back inside my head. I was only 12 yrs. old. But even back then, I views life, like a game of baseball. Where I was at bat. Having 3 balls and 2 strikes already against me and, the next pitch. Would determine, how I would go out in life.

Fast forward,

Although most folkes in my neighborhood call me Tim.; My full first name is Timothy. Much like SAY-SAY, whom real name is Sarah. Say-say, ours 13 yrs old character's. Had a powerful appetite for sex. Which led my writing to some Strong–Lan–Guges.

That censure me, to fill in the blank. In many of her episode occurrence

Fast-forward,

Racial profiling and numerous killing of black men. By red-neck whites. Had a lot to contribute to SAY-SAY emotional behaviors_ _ _that alternately bewitched SARAH to Nym-pholepsy's!

After numerous black men were killed; Dozens of demonstrations, and sit-ins. SAY-SAY finally came into her own. Tho, she still was pledge with Nympholepsy's she and Timothy were marry. Later, she went on to become a leading civil rights activates.

Timothy became a U. S. congressman for the 5th district and, was one of first black; to run for president.

_ _ _Warning, Colored Peoples! The book wasn't written political-correct! _ _ _Through-out our's story; I provide a narrative commentary. Outside the box!

__CHAPTER – ONE__

NARRATOR_ Shortly after this commercial ship had blocked in this Charleston harbor. Carrying a large cargo of African's slaves. I saw hundreds of black people; Being herded into a nearby warehouse.

From the looks upon their faces. Many seem so—over whelm; From their long voyage. Coming across the sea! They were cramped–up! Like animals in a cargo, standing room only!

I could only imagine their frustrations. And I saw some of theirs naked fleshs! That had been stains with regurgitated fluid. From their fellow slaves who were too sick to continue their journey. At day break I saw that same group being herded back out front.

This time, they were grouped into numbers; That total the sum of fingers, on one hand. While being ushered up onto a flat tree like platform.

Where a group of white men stood roundabout waiting to negotiate theirs bids, to purchase ower-ship of us slaves!

Minuters later,

Ten fingers total of us slaves; Were chains-tied together. And quickly led away by ours new master. To an inland place called, 'Columbia'_ _ _

After two days of traveling through swamp and snakes effective land. We arrived at a back wood littler plantation. There, we were greeted by a slow-talking white OVER–SEE-ER'S: "_ _ _Now listen up!" He yelled "_ _ _You people are now the property of Master CLARKSON! For the next 40 summers! To work off your debts – to the bank! And I. (He pointed) be your boss OVER–SEE-ER'S! – From sun–up–till the sun goes down!!"

NARRATORS_ This CLARKSON plantation was a living night-mare! – working in an environment of mosquitos and extreme heat! In a field where this OVER–SEE-ER'S took pleasure in using his whip!

From the start, all male slaves were housed in separate quarters. Away from our sisters and mothers! There were no communicating allowed among males and females – slaves.

After 14 hours, working the field each day. Severals field-hands from the CLARKSON'S Plantation. Began a ritualism – ceremony with drums — communicating with ours African brothers. Miles away, At the SIM'S Plantation. Drums – beats: '_ _ _Many/of ours/Africans – sisters – mothers too/now big/with – child/white – Master's/child_ _ _!'

Narrators__ The sounds, coming out of the mid-night-air. Reveal a catastrophe most disturbance! Alarming as it is; having such large number of pregnancy's of female slaves. Almost at the same time. Were mind-boggling! – Not to count the large number of mix breed childrens.

Fast–forward

These half white and half black childrens. Grew – up, re-fusing to live theirs lifes as slaves! Soon, they began to rebel and became known as the fore-runner's of the civil rights movement!

_ _ _Their rebelious came during the presidency's of Mr. Linclon. Their movement were parallel to the controversial promise! (40 acres and a mule). These offsprings continue their rebellion through the administration of Pres. Johnson – Grant and R. Hoyes! Then to President J. A. Garfield, Pres. C. A. Arthur, President C. Clevland. Onto President B. Harrison, Pres. T. Rossevelt, Pres W. Taft, Pres W. Wilson, Pres. W. Harding. Onto an era of world – war one!

Theirs movement didn't stop there TT continue through Pres C. Coolidge. President H.Hoover. All the way to president F. D. Roosevelt; and his new deal onto world war two!

Their uprising seem to intensify. Starting with the administration of Pres. Truman, President D. Eisenhower, Pres, J. Kennedy's. All the way to President L. Johnson. Where theirs up-rising erupted into the passing of the Civil – Rights Acts of 1964-65 and bb_ _ _!

Narrators: After the passing of those three Civil – Rights Acts. Ours adventurous–story took its beginning_ _ _

The rushing white water cease it's running raids. Into a mild lazy lake. There, the water line thrust in ward kissing the sandy white sand. That displayed a welcome – mat right before my eyes. In the mid – of, hundreds of college students. _ _ _ After all, today is the opening of spring – break!

Alternately, it was by sheer luck. I saw this young girl. Coming out of an apartment. High – up on a hill side. That over-looks this small water front community.

From here, her hair was push back into two long braids. Her face, Majestically portrays two high cheeks. That curved into a beautiful smile.

She couldn't have been a day over 15 yrs. old! Yet, from her neck down. Her body artistically curve into two mountains of fleshs! That was well perportion for her littler petite frame.

As she walk, she began imitating a fews dance steps. From the music that was playing in the back ground.

Unfortunately, this predominat blk neighborhood. According to government standards. Was well below the poverty level and, for a group of people! So poverty-stricken! Could have some impact while this large crowd of demonstrators were here today.

_ _ _Meanwhile, as the student gather. The local chapter of the N.A.A.C.P. coordinators was there coordinating the action! Listen now as the crowd marchs along the water front "_ _ _we shall overcome – we shall overcome – we shall over–come! we shall overcome – one day_ _ _"

As they sing, I casually walked – up where this young lady was now dancing and say: "_ _ _Hi beautiful! What's going on??_ _ _" She look surprise, smiling she reply. "_ _ _You sir!" There was brief pause before I said. "_ _ _Pretty lady, you got a name?" – She snap and said. "_ _ _My name is Sarah – Sir! – But, most of my friends call me Say-Say!"

Moving foreward, now extending my hand. I whisper "_ _ _My name is Timothy! – But most of my friend just call me Tim!" I whisper. Pausing agan before saying. "…Say-Say! Are you going down to joins the demonstrators??" I ask.

She snap and say "_ _ _No Sir! My old father's won't let me go!" She then pause agan before saying. "_ _ _Sir! How old do you think I am?", She ask.

I hesitated before uttering. "…Oh!!" She interrupte me saying. "_ _ _I am thirteen going on 14 yrs. old!" I shouted. "_ _ _You're kidding me!", I whisper smiling now, she said "_ _ _Oh! – You thought I was older, because of these!" She pointed toward her over size breasts. I snap and said "_ _ _No!!"

She interrupte me again and said. "_ _ _Come on Sir! – Most men when I first meet them. Always look at my body; And think I am older!" She whisper.

Suddenly, a deep – loud voice yelled – out from inside her apartment "_ _ _Say-Say! Stop flirting with that man; and bring your ass in the house!" This voice ordered.

She jumped before saying: "_ _ _Coming momma! (Pause)_ _ _Oh Sir! I got to go but if you're sure you want to talk to a young chick! Like me call me!" Reaching, she gaved me a small strip of paper with her number on it. Before rushing into her apartment.

_ _ _Minutes later. I made my way down near the water front and found the demonstrator's a lilttler more organized. They were parading back and forth like soldier's ants.

Looking just beyound the demonstrators. I saw a mass Cumulus – cloud – of smog. Suspended over the water, I shook my head. when I read the words on one of theirs signs; "_ _ _ We're sick and tired of being pissed all on by whites!!?

The demonstrators then amplify theirs sing-ing: "_ _ _We don't want no – body – to give us noth-ing! – Just open – in – up the door! – and we will – get it – our-selves! – we don't want no-body – to give us nothing just –open _ _ _".

When I heard and saw theirs littler theatrical marchs – step! I was impressed, and knew I wanted to joined theirs marchs!

Just then, the group change course. And start maching up near the front of Woolworth and kress stores. As we marchs now sing-ing in a slow tem-per: "_ _ _We shall – overcome! we shall overcome!! – we shall overcome – one day_ _ _!!!"

While marching ours group into the waiting present. Of a large unit of white policemen. All combat ready! Suddenly, this chief of policeman shouted. While standing amid his cruser.

"_ _ _You people! Are all trust passing on public property! – You have no rights here!!"

The marcher's start sing-ing even louder. I notice this chief face appearing a redest – orange from his nose down. He shouted: "_ _ _I am gona give you'll one minutes to disband and vacate or be arrested!!", he yelled.

The volume of sing-ing got even louder. Just then, all hell broked loose. In a stampede. Severals N.B.C. camera – men were ran over! – Many demonstrators were tackle and brutally placed hands cuffs! – Thrown in the rear of severals city sanitation trucks and carry off to jail.

On ours way to jail. Although it was pitch dark. In the rear of a garage truck. We began sing-ing: "_ _ _Oh freedom! – Oh freedom!! – Oh freedom – over me my lord! – Before – I be a slave! – I'll be bury – in my grave! – and go home to my lord! – and be free."

Narrators: The words of ours song express the conditions of how we had been treated. As a people! Enslaved by the very race of people who found this country on that creed: "_ _ _We hold these truths – to be self-evident; That all men are created equally!"

_____And, it's all being watch on a world's – stage! On national television. That day, so many demonstrators were arrested. They didn't have enough jail cells I was among the first waves; to be jail. I was jammed in a small six by 12 fts cell; Alone with five other. While many of the 2nd wave were hand – cuffs alone the railing in the hallways.

_____There were so many demonstrators arrested. The local newspaper and television station were having a field day! In fact, one news – commentator's reported saying:

"_ _ _Before good white folkes yield to niggers! As our's equal! – All hell will freeze over first!!"

_____Meanwhile, inside that crowded cell. I was in a discussion with another cellmate. "_ _ _My brother! I take you're not from around here?", He ask.

I reply, "_ _ _I am attending college just across the way at A.T.v.T. – But, no I am from up north!" I whisper

He shouted "_ _ _North or South, My brother! – The entire U.S. is all Jim – crows country. When it comes to blk folkes!"

"_ _ _I didn't re-alize it was this bad down here!" I whisper.

He reply, "_ _ _Colored folks have been lock up in shit – houses like this every since I can remember_ _ _!"

Shaking my head, I then whisper: "_ _ _ That's a damn shame!" Smiling he said: "_ _ _My brother! This is a white man worlds! We've got to try living in it _ _ _"

_____After five days in jail. That first group. Which was arrested. Were brought before a magistrate court. To my surprise, we were represented by an attorney from the N.A A.C.P. who argue ours case saying; ours arrest were un-constitutional! "_ _ _ Your honor! The arrest of each my clients; Is un-constitutional!!", This attorney shouted.

This judge reply: "_ _ _So you don't believe all these boys are guilty?" Judge ask.

This N.A.A.C.P. Attorney countered.

"_ _ _Your honor! They committed no crime! They were demonstrating against your Jim – Crows Laws!"

This judge reply: "These ass-holes were parading without a permit!"

N. A. A. C P. Attorney ask: "_ _ _So, you're gona Lock-up all these people. For walking around on a public street?", this attorney ask.

Judge snap – saying: "_ _ _I've heard enough from you! – I fined each of them S. O. B.! 25 – dollars – cased closed…"

Narrators: I was relief after paying my $25 fined walking across the street. I decided to call that young girl; I met that first day: "_ _ _May I speak to Sarah please!", I ask – when a voice on the other end Say "_ _ _This is Sarah speaking Sarah Sir!" She whisper.

I then tried to explain: " _ _ _Sarah – honey! – I am the young man you met on your front porch! – the other day. I am glad your mother's wouldn't let you go down and joined those demonstrators! – I did, and I was thrown in Jail!"

Say-Say reply: "_ _ _I know, I saw you on T.V. while they were putting you in the rear of the trash – truck! – are you ok??" She ask.

I answered: "_ _ _I am fine now, I just got out! – oh! Sarah could you meet me down at the student center, on campus?", I ask.

Say-Say reply: "_ _ _Yes, I think I can slip away!" She whisper.

Tim said: "_ _ _Good! Then I will see you in 20 minutes!" Tim whisper.

Narrators: I rushs out of that phone booth; Into a monstrous crowd. Watching the independence – day parade I miss the first cross town bus.

When I did arrived on campus. I made my way through a pedestrians group of students. All moving around like soldiers – ants. It was then, I saw Say-Say from a distance. Approaching her I greeted her saying: "…Hi pretty lady! Have you been waiting long?", I ask.

She answered: "_ _ _No Sir! I just got here!", she whisper.

I then ask: "_ _ _would you liked to go inside?", I ask.

Narrators: Once inside the student's lounge. Say-Say and I sit at one of those vacant love seats. That was set-up around a large screen television.

In fact the President was just beginning to address the nation. From the white house. On all of the civil rights demonstrations!

Say-Say quickly ask: "_ _ _Mister Tim – could you turn that up?"

I was shock, I reply: "_ _ _Don't tell me young lady; you're into current events?", I ask.

She reply: "_ _ _Oh yes Sir! – There's a crazy white world out there; and black folks need to be abreast on what's going on!" She whisper.

Narrators: I started to comment before the President began speaking: "_ _ _I can't give no sweeping opinion on all these sit-ins strikes of negros. Protesting lunch counters – segregation!

_ _ _But I am deeply sympathetic with the efforts of any group to enjoy the rights of equality – guaranteed by the constitution. (Pause)_ _ _If every city and every community of the south held bi-racial problems. This would be much better then a national conferences to help settle racial – problems _ _ _This would be much better then a national – conferences _ _ _ (he ended)

Say-Say face was blood – red! Immediately after the President speech Gov. Nelson Rockerfeller follow with a stronger comment: "_ _ _All these sit-ins are an inspiring example of ours nation_ _ _and our civil rights problems – could be solved by moral force and appeal of human conscience. Personified by young men and women – who sit at those segregated lunch counters_ _ _"

Narrators: After hearing both the president and Mr.Rocker-feller's. I turned to Say-Say and whisper:

"_ _ _Sarah! I am not convince now! That all theses demonstrations are worst it! – (Pause) If these whites folkes don't want us eating at their lunch counters! – I. for one could be cool with that!"

When I mention this to Say-Say it was like, I had lit-up a fire-cracker! She shouted: "_ _ _Tim! It's not just the eating part! – It's the got – damn – prin-cipal! – cain't you see that?" Startle, I shook my head in dis-belief and ask: "_ _ _Honey! how did you get so – wise at thirteen??", I ask.

Dis-regarding my question, she reply: "_ _ _Mister Tim! Do you remember that incident where this white – pig – fu – they interview on C.B.S? It was his intention to start a revolution. To put all blacks folkes on boats; and ship us back to Africa!"

Shaking my head in aggrement I reply: "_ _ _I believe you're right!! If I could remember correctly – He was that shit – ass! That kid-napped another black brother; and drove him out in an open field – where he beat that brother with a tire – iron! – carved the letters, K.K.K on his chest! – And hunged him to a tree!!"

Sobbing now Say-Say whisper: "_ _ _Tim! He was killed all because he was black! he began to openly cry.

I whisper: "_ _ _You're even more beautiful when you cry!!" I cited.

She then ask: "_ _ _Mister Tim! – Is this that part in Shakepeare's play; where Romeo kisses Juliet??" She ask.

Her question caught me by surprise. I mumble: "_ _ _Yes my love, this is that part; Where I – Romeo! Would love to kiss you – Juliet!!", I whisper

She utter with a giggle – saying: "_ _ _Mr. Tim! I never kiss a man before!" While putting the palms of her hands over her eyes."

Spontaneously, I reach over and gently smack her on her lip. She applaud with a loud cheer!

"_ _ _Wowww_ _ _"

Right there, in the mid of this crowded lounge. Ours lips reunite. Caressing – passionly! And almost as quickly, she push me away and whisper: "_ _ _Mister Tim! – I think I am gona faint! – There's a whirl – wind moving about in my head!", she whis-per.

I mimic saying: "_ _ _Think you're gona faint?". I ask.

She began explaining: "_ _ _Yes, that's a temporary decrease of blood; Being supply to the brains!", She said.

Shaking my head I utter: "_ _ _Young lady! You're much too advance to be thirteen!?" While squeezing her hand I added. "_ _ _Miss Sarah! The reason I ask you to meet me here today. (I pause) is to get to know you better. And to see could I be your only man! – (I pause again) _ _ _I realized you're young! – But, what I've witness here today! Is, you're more mature then the aver1age 20 yrs. old woman! – (pause again))_ _ _Miss Sarah! would you have me to be your man?", I ask.

She reply: "_ _ _Yes, Yes! Mister Tim, I knew you was the man for me; every since that first day you walked up on me_ _ _" she whisper I smiled and end – saying: "_ _ _Then it's a done deal! – Me for you – and you for me – forever_ _ _"

Narrators: Racial tensions had clouded this city like a hot bed of fermenting manure Jim Crows laws had been thee dominant – rule; over this Negros neighborhood.

Drive-by shooting of black men were on the rise today, two whites cops were on patrol; In this south side poverty littler community. As they drove up alongside this black man. On this deserted dead end street; who was smoking a jointed.

Both cops jump out their patrol car with guns drawn. The first cop shouted: "_ _ _Boy! Get out of that car, and put your hands – up!" – The other then ask. "_ _ _Boy what are you doing back here on this deserted road?" 2nd cop ask.

This black man answer: "_ _ _Officers! I am not gona lie to you; I was smoking this jointed"

The first cop said: "_ _ _Boy don't you know, that smoking marijuana is against the law?" He pause before saying "_ _ _It makes you niggers crazy!!"

The first cop said to the second cop and whisper: "_ _ _Charlie, I think this boy need to be taught a lesson!"

Both cops then commence shooting; empty-ing their revolver's into this blk. man. Just then, a voice from the house on corner yelled: "_ _ _Hey! you two I saw that! You'll just killed an un-armed man! – old joe, didn't have a chance!"

_____Both cops rushs over to the front side house yard. Where this voice was coming from. And ask: "_ _ _What's your name? And what is it, you seen?"

This voice snap – and say: "_ _ _I saw two, son-er – a – bitches! shooting that poor brother for no reason at all!!", This voice shouted.

The 1st cop then said: "_ _ _Charlie! I think we just found ours mur-ders! who killed that nigger over there_ _ _"

This 2nd cop add, saying: "…Boy! you're under arrest for the murder of…"

_____Shit like this happen all the time. Crooked cops. Making fraudulent arrests. Just to cover theirs asses! Today, another black life gone!

___CHAPTER – TWO___

Narrators: All across the United States; Ethnic – discrimination were being experiencing. B.K.O., Blacks – Killings – Operation – Officer's. We're shooting and killings blacks men at an alarming rate!

White segregationer's had intensify theirs practices of segregation. Jim – crow laws were here to stay! At the time, the N.A.A.C.P had organize a group of freedom riders. To ride through the south; To test the interstate commerce rule.

Whites folkes were coming out of the wood-works to protest, today, the Grayhound bus station was un-usually crowed. For a Saturday morning. Whites had flooded the waiting section all were waiting for the arrival of the first phase. (bus – load) of freedom riders; coming from the north.

Just across the street. I saw a small group of policemen along with K-9's dogs. All anxiously – waiting. Parked on the shoulders of the street was a large television news truck. Already broad-casting: "_ _ _ This is news break! – Today, the federal – inter-state commerce – transportations. Is being challenge! – We're waiting on the arrival of the first phase of freedom riders!"

_____Directly in front of the station. Dozens of Klansmen were now marching, carry-ing signs which read: "_ _ _Niggers and dogs are not allowed — white-power forever – niggers go back north! – segregation now and forever! _ _ _"

Grayhound was located in that section of town. Near the edge of soul town where a half dozens black business – operate.

Fifty feets inside of soul town was a colored – establishment. That call themselves, Moon – Glo – Café a urban littler restaurant; which was no more then a – small – hole in the wall that was known for serving such dishes: '_ _ _Corn bread, black – eyes – peas! – collar green and ham-hocks – where the meat was cook til it fell off the bone.'

Narrators: This morning moon Glo was abnormally crowded. Maybe, because of all the excitement in town today.

Three men were sitting up front; in view of the bus station. At a large picture window. All flabber – gastings about what was unfolding, up at the bus station.

The first man reply: "_ _ _Tell me, what do you think about that sign (he pointed) – up there!"

The other man responds: "_ _ _Are you talking about that sign (he pointed) – that say: "Niggers and dogs are not allowed!

The first man then ask: "_ _ _I wonder why them buck-ler's hate us so?" Then the man with the loudest mouths. Shouted: "_ _ _I'll tell you why! Everytime one of them white look at us; they always see a littler bit of themselves in us!"

_____They were talking so loud, everyone began to take notice. It was then, that the other man said: "_ _ _Now – AR – dats, there ain't no such person! Being 100% negro anymore!!"

The 1st man said: "_ _ _Yes uncle – Charlies been f...k.g around with ours black women for years!"

All three men start laughing. When the 1st man shouted: "_ _ _No, no, that ain't the only reason theses whites men don't want us niggers; getting next to his women! Most white men cain't measure to up to us!"

The other man stood – up and shouted: "_ _ _Yes, yes! why settle for littler pork sausages! When theirs women can enjoys large polish – sausage!"

The entire cafe – group start laughing just before the excitements shift back-up at the grayhound station.

Narrrator's: The grayhound bus pulled into the terminal amid a hostile crowd. That was screaming angry insults: "_ _ _Don't get off the bus! – segregation now forever! – Niggers and dogs are not allowed!"

_____When the first group step off the bus; They were met by a steady force of pushing and shoving. The first freedom riders was thrown to the ground and attack by dogs.

Like puppet, each freedom riders came under attack. In the most bloody and violent manner. Blood was pouring onto the sidewalk, like raindrops!

While all this was going on. I saw those same three men, from the café. Walking toward a black pick-up truck. That was parked out front of the café.

They then, position themselves belly–down. In the truck bed covering themselves with a canvas; with the tailgate pulled-up. There appeared, three small opening just large enough to focus three high power rifles.

_____Backup at ground-zero; amid those rebellions group of opposition. Someone hurls a cock-tail bomb. Up, on the bus. Causing a mushroom like cloud – explosion into the air. Body – parts, from thoses passenger's, still on the bus. Were scatter everywhere.

Back, in the rear-bed of this pickup truck. Theses three men began taking pot shots at theirs targets! Policemen, Klansmen even K-9's. Began falling like littler toys soldiers!

It appeared that their weapons were muffler with silents devices which made it difficult for the policemen, Klansmen – group. To determine where the shots were coming from.

I had myself a front row seat sitting alone at that same table. Those three men had been sitting. Just then, a voice ask: "_ _ _Are you ready to placed your order? ...Seem like you're watching a good ole – shoot – em – up!"

I whisper: "_ _ _It's more like an animal – slaughters!! (Then I lied) – but, I don't see where all them shots are coming from!"

This waitress frowned and say: "_ _ _Nigger please! – I am no detectors and I know where these shots are coming from! (Pointing) – right there, from that pick-up truck!"

I lied again saying; "_ _ _No shit!!"

Agan she reply: "_ _ _Nigger, are you ready to order??"

I then answered: "_ _ _Oh yes, may I have an order of ox – tails over rice – collard green, corn bread. And a side order of potatoes salad!"

Smiling she said: "_ _ _Home boy, all that shooting must have made you hungry!"

While walking away I call after her and say: "_ _ _Oh Miss! would you take this quarter and re-play that last song."

Narrator's: Back up at ground zero. Those policemen, who manage to escape without being shot. Were running about like their heads were cut-off. Severals emergencys vehicles had now block the west bound traffic while medical personals pick-up those dead – corpse.

Suddenly, the volume on the juke – box sounded '_ _ _Don't know much about history! Don't know much about the French – I took! – But, I do know, that I love you and I know – if you love me too! – What – ar – wonder-ful world this would be_ _ _"

_____After the record had end. I saw those three men rushing away from the rear of that pick-up truck and ran back into the cafe. While walking up to my table. The man with the loudest mouths shouted: "_ _ _ Hey youngblood! I think you're sitting at our's table! – May we share, it with you?"

I look-up and motion – saying: "_ _ _Have some sit down!!" I utter some of my geechee talks!

Then the 1st man ask: "_ _ _Have you been sitting here long?"

I reply: "_ _ _Sir, I've been sitting here long enough to eat a whole meal – but, I ain't seen a thing. I've been too busy eating_ _ _"

The first man then said: "_ _ _Boy you sound like you got a littler geecher in you! But you're my kind-of nigger!"

Reaching across the table. This 1st man said: "_ _ _I am Joseph Jackson, (Pointing) He's David Dessausure and that fellow there is Samuel Petterson!

"_ _ _Yes, we're down here from the Chicago branch of the black – panther's!", He cited.

I asked: "_ _ _ What bring you – panthers! This far south?" I ask.

The other man answer: "_ _ _We were hoping on setting up a local chapter of panther's, down here!" He reply.

Our conversation came to an abrupt end. When to uniform cops enter. All three men casually got-up and walked out. I went back to humming the words of the song: '_ _ _What – ar – wonder-ful – world this – would be_ _ _'

While humming, this waitress came back to my table and ask: "_ _ _How well do you know Say-Say?" She ask – she caught me by surprise, I snap and said. "_ _ _You know my girl Say-Say!"

This waitdress then said: "_ _ _Sir! This is a very small blk neighborhood! – I saw you just last week, walking with Say-Say in city – park. She and my baby sister are in the same 8th grade class!"

Surprisingly I said: "_ _ _What – a – coincidence, yes she's my girl! – what else do you know about Say-Say?"

She said: "_ _ _I know sir! she is way too young for you, even tho, she may have a mature looking body_ _ _". Upon walking away.

Leaving Moon – Glo cafe. I made a pit stop over at the post – office to have some postals printed onto. My meter, one of my weekly duties; as mail clerk. For the college. Thinking out loud: '_ _ _At lease, this scholar – ship – aid job help pay my way through school.'

Coming out of the post – office. I met Say-Say and a very familiars looking older – man. I hail her firs: "_ _ _Hey Miss Sarah!" Trying to be as polite as possible.

She look an voiced: "_ _ _Hi Mister Timothy (pause) this is my father."

Extending my hand. I said: "_ _ _Please to meet you sir!"

Frowning, he asked: "_ _ _Young man, where do I know you from??"

I whisper: "_ _ _Sir, could it be. I was one of those demonstrator's that was arrested last week!"

Smiling now, he said: "_ _ _That's where I saw your face on T.V being put into the rear of a garbage truck – keep – the good work up, young man!

Now walking away Say-Say turn and yelled: "_ _ _Mr. Timothy, would you call me later?"

At the bus stop, I kepted racking my brain's 'where have I seen Say-Say father's from?_ _ _ That's it, he's the field directors for the N.A.A.C.P and he was in court along with that attorney last week.

Narrator's: The entire city was under – going rapid changes – tension between blacks and whites had stretch to a raw edge. And after that mass killings; Fews days ago, this city was like ticking – time – bomb! Just waiting, for more to happen.

_____Later that evening, at my dorm room. I turn the small television set to the 6:00 – clock news: "_ _ _Good evening!! – This is the N.B.C 6:00 o'clock news – today 7 policemen, 5 firemen, 8 Klansmen and 3 K-9's dogs! were killed by snipers bullets – from an unknown source – near the Grayhound bus station in down town Greensboro!– That's the headlines – I'll have more in just a minutes_ _ _!"

Just then my cellphone ring. It was Say-Say: "_ _ _What's up!" I shouted thru the phone.

She shouted back: "_ _ _Tim! Turn your T.V to the 6:00 news!"

I said: "_ _ _Honey, I am ahead of you, I have it on!"

She hesitated before saying: "_ _ _ This segregation thing, is getting serious! Anyway, I won't be able to see you tonight. But could we please meet somewhere, on tomorrow, maybe over, some soda – pop?"

I said: "_ _ _Sure we can! If you would catch the 12:10 blue line bus; coming down town on tomorrow! – I will already be on the bus! – so until then, good-bye!"

_____The news contine: '_ _ _After this mass killing today! E.B.E directors announced his intention of going to North Carolina to personnal oversee this investigations_ _ _'

Narrator's: Twenty–four hours later. I caught the 12:10 south bound bus. And took a seat just to the rear of the back door. Although the bus was near empty. I was fully aware of Jim – Crow law. Which specific – forbid Negros from sitting in the front of the bus.

Severals bus stops later. Say-Say step – up on the bus. She was greeted flirtatiously by this white driver: "_ _ _Morning Miss sunshine!" He loudly echo.

Before Say-Say spoked – back. I yelled out: "_ _ _Say-Say, I am back here!!"

Casually, she spoked: "_ _ _Morning Sir!"

When she got back. Where I was sitting I said out loud: "_ _ _It look like that driver's was flirting with you!!"

Say-Say said out loud: "_ _ _Look Tim! I don't get down with white men like that!"

I then reply: "_ _ _Good! For a while there I thought I might had to go up there; and whip his ass!!!"

Just then, this driver's yelled – back: "_ _ _What – did – say, boy?"

Before I could respond Say-Say put her hand over my mouth and shouted back: "_ _ _There ain't no boy back here!!"

This driver's countered: "_ _ _ Gal! You people are all a – like! Won't let someone be nice to you; without putting your ass on your shoulders!"

I made an attempt to go up front. When Say-Say caution me, saying: "_ _ _Tim! Don't go up there! That shit-ass ain't worst it"

I whisper: "_ _ _Maybe you're right! He not worst going to jail for!"

Minutes later Say-Say and I exit the bus. At the corner by the Grayhound station. Right in the middle of a group of civil rights demonstrator's. That were marching saying and sing-ing: "_ _ _Say it loud! – Say it loud!! – Say – it – loud!!! – I am black and I am proud! – Say it_ _ _"

Say-Say grabbed me by my arm and ask: "_ _ _Have you ever eaten over here?"

I shouted: "_ _ _Yes, Moon – Glo is a very popular eating spot for the black folkes!!"

Almost screaming, she said: "_ _ _Ok then let's go there!"

Pushing ours way through the demonstrator's. Minutes later, we enter the restaurant and took a table, the second row from the entrence, Immediately, after we were seated. That same waitress walked over and greeted us: "_ _ _Well hello there handsome!!" she whisper to me.

Before I was able to respond Say-Say shouted: "_ _ _Oh hell no bitch! Are you getting fresh with my man?"

This waitress then snap – saying: "_ _ _Looker here littler girl! I was just complementing your man!"

Say-Say echo saying: "_ _ _Complementing my ass!"

This waitress then ask: "_ _ _What-ever, what can I get you – two??"

I interrupt and said: "_ _ _May we have two mtn.dew on the rock!"

Say-Say interrupt and reply: "_ _ _No bitch, give me mine in the can; I don't trust you bitch!"

_____After this waitress left, I reached across the table and whisper: "_ _ _Honey, there's no need for you to be jealous! Remember ours littler agreement? – Me –for – you! And you – for me!"

Frowning now, Say-Say ask: "_ _ _Ok then, if you're mine! When will you make me a woman?"

Hesitantly, I said: "_ _ _Sarah honey! I don't think your littler body; is ready for that yet!"

Speaking loud: "_ _ _Tim! Got damned, I am a big girl! Please don't insult my intelligence!"

I then whisper: "_ _ _Sarah, that wasn't my intention beside, if was caught making love to you. They would get me for satutory rape!"

She reply: "_ _ _That's not true! Not if the women consent to having sex!"

I said: That – just – it, even if you do give consent, Sarah in the eyes of the law, you are still a child!"

Raising her voice agan, she shouted: "_ _ _That just ain't fair!!

I reply: I know honey, but that's the law!"

She looked across the table with tears in her eyes. She ask: "_ _ _Can you just overlook this law, this one time?"

I said: "_ _ _Honey, I wish we could!"

Having said that, she lower her littler body under the table and beg: "_ _ _Please, pretty – please!?? While pullingonto my belt – buckers.

Embarrass, I whisper: "_ _ _Say-Say come from under that table, before someone sees you!!"

Coming from under the table she yelled: "_ _ _Tim – o – thy! God – damned, I want to f_ _ _!!??

The waitdress overheard Say-Say while coming back to ours table. She echo: " _ _ _Nasty – ass –heifer's!!"

Say-Say then shouted: "_ _ _You agan bitch! How about can-celling ours order! Were leaving!!"

This waitdress yelled: "_ _ _You cain't just leave like that littler girl!"

Say-Say shouted: "_ _ _Watch me bitch! Tim Let's get the hell out of here!"

Narrator's: When Say-Say and I left Moon-Glo. The demonstrator's crowd had intensify.

There were uniform cops present all along the streets. We start walking in the direction of confederate – city park. A just recently integrated – piece of recreation grounds. That was first establish, shortly after the civil war.

According to records, this park was erected to commenrate. All those brave white soldiers. Who fought to preserve segregation. Today, although all of the confederate statues had been remove. City – officials retain it's name, confederate – park.

_____It was near dark when Say-Say and I reach the entrance of the park. While walking up under the tall confederate-flag pole. I whisper:

"Say-Say, do you think it's safe to enter?" Say-Say answered – saying. "_ _ _Hell yes! Who's going to stop us?" Nervously I echo. "The police for one! And any other segregationer's that might pass by _ _ _"

_____While continue walking, we took a seat. At the first set of benches. There Say-Say continue talking "Tim, do you know how many days. It took the N.A.A.C.P. to demonstrate, to get this park in-tegated??" She ask.

I answer: "_ _ _Say-Say! I don't' have the slightest ideal!!" Say-Say then said: "_ _ _Well I'll tell you! – my father, John Henry Joyner lead a crew of demonstrators out here 66 days! – And many a days, I was right out here with him_ _ _ "

I reply: "_ _ _ That's amazing!!" She continue " _ _ _My Dad once told me about a similar integration incident – about a white – swimming pool!!"

I asked: "_ _ _ A swimming pool?" She then whisper "_ _ _Yes, a swimming pool! – Before those white folkes gaved – in! – And allowed blacks to swim in their pool. City councilmens order that the pool be fill with dirt – and made into a flower – garden!"

I whisper: "_ _ _Humm – there are some sick whites folkes, out here!"

Narrator's: Say-Say had a wealth – of knowledges, on the integration being the daughters of, N.A.A.C.P. field directors. She went on talking about another integration incident: "_ _ _There was another group of Negros college students. That got together one Sunday morning. And decided to attend services. At this all white church. Where they approach the front door. The usher's refuse to let them in! That was when this students leader said to the usher:

'Jesus – Christ once came to the door of a church like your and they refused to let him in. How do you not know: That Christ is not coming this time as a group of Negros – students like us_ _'

Tim asked: "_ _ _What kind of answer, this ushers gaved them?

Say-Say answer: "_ _ _ He didn't, But that next Sunday. They went back to the door of that church and was allowed to enter_ _ _"

_____Say-Say and I sit on that park bench that night for hours. I couldn't help from see-ing how beautiful she look.

Her Body had blossen out like a flower. Her face picture, all of the elegances – of a mature woman. I change subject and whisper: "_ _ _Say-Say! If you knew how much I love you!"

She then said: "_ _ _Tim, every since that first time when I met you, I haven't question your love for me! My only concern now! – When will you man – up! And make me a woman??"

Before answering, a uniform cop walked up to us and shouted: "What in – the hell! Are you – people doing out here?"

Say-Say whisper: "_ _ _We're just sitting officer"

This cop then ask: "Have you'll seen two colored boys; running through here?" This cop ask.

Say-Say snap – saying: "_ _ _We wasn't looking!!" She said, minutes before this cop walked away.

_____The next few minutes we spend gazing at that full moon. Reminiscing ours love for each other. She broked ours moment of silent: "_ _ _Show me how you love me!"

Reaching over, I pulled her into my arms. Kissing her passionately our bodies became inseparable. Until a voice interrupt: "_ _ _You two need to get the hell out of this park; and fine yourselves a colored – motel somewhere! _ _ _That's an order!!!" This voice belong to that same white cop. Whom had been by earlier. Immediately, we rushs out of the park. And went to catch the north-bound blue line bus_ _ _.

_____45 minutes later, I walk into my dorm's room humming the melody: "_ _ _I – am in love – with an angle! I am – on my way to heaven!!"

Inside my room I found my room-mate. Watching the 2nd game. The cowboys were beating – up on the redskins. I greeted him.

I shouted: "_ _ _What's up!!" He quickly reply: "_ _ _You, my nigger! (pause) you sound extremely happy. Did that pretty littler thing; finally gave you some?"

I shook my head and said: "_ _ _No, ain't nothing like that!"

He then change the subject and say: "_ _ _I've been messing with this old – ass woman. Who has been paying me to give her some! (he brag).

I reply: "_ _ _No – shit! I knew you was sleeping around with this marry woman. But, she been paying you?" (I ask).

He shouted: "Hell yes, she claim that her husband is impotent suffering from hyper – tension!"

I ask: " _ _ _ And you don't feel bad about getting over on this brother?"

He frown and then shouted: "_ _ _Hell no, it ain't my fault; He cain't get it up!"

I said: "_ _ _You do know, that high blood pressure; is something that occur most commonly with black men?"

He reply: "_ _ _Look, my brother, please don't go – lecturing me! Ayway, she have a pretty – littler daughters! Maybe, I could hook you up with!"

I held both hands – up and shouted: "_ _ _No thank brut! I am – straight!" I said.

Narrator: Because of all the killings. A.T and T. Had sanction a dusk – to – dawn curfew. This race problems had gotten entangle so – complex! That both side, blk. And whites; were at the brim of destruction!

Blacks were facing a melting – pot of problems! Theirs young men, had to fear; being shot and killed by white policemen! And then there was this chronic disease. That attack only blacks! A bodily – disorder of high blood pressure, hypertension and heart ailment!

All, became the black – man number one enemy. Next to Jim – Crows , was ethnic cleansing!

Early in the next morning. Shortly before 7: AM Say-say call, she sound trouble.

"_ _ _Tim are you busy? – I need someone to talk to! Could you meet me in 20 minutes over at the seven – eleven?" She ask.

I reply: "_ _ _Of course I can!"

_____7/11 was less then a twenty minutes walk away. It was right across the interstate from campus. When I arrived in the front parking lot – of the store. Say-Say was sitting on the drivers side of a well kepted 55's Chevrolet.

Walking up, I greeted her while getting in on the passenger's side. I reply: "_ _ _Honey, I didn't know you had a drivers – license?"

Say–Say reply: "_ _ _I don't, but I can drive! (pause) Tim, what your opinion on a stay – at home mom! That drives the family only car! And she refuse to let my fathers drive! (Sobbing now) He has to catch the bus everywhere he go!" She began openly – crying.

I reply: "_ _ _Honey, I think that's a shame!"

Say-Say continue: "_ _ _And last night, they argues all night long!" She cry.

I reply agan: "_ _ _That's definitely not good"

Say-Say continue: "_ _ _From what I could hear through the wall! My momma kepted saying 'Man you're weak – in the bedroom! You're pushing me out into the arms of other men!"

I snap and say: "_ _ _Your mom, said that to him?" I ask.

Say-Say continue: "_ _ _Wait, there's more! My father's kepted saying. '_ _ _Honey, I cain't control that! It's my high – blood pressure – medication! Its cuts my nature!!" He tried to explain.

_____My mother's wasn't hearing any of that. I then heard her Yelled: "_ _ _That's not my problem – nigger! I need some love right now! If I cain't get it from you! I'll get it from another man!"

I whisper: "_ _ _That mother – of – your, is bold! Some men would have knock – her, on her ass!" I said.

Say-Say then reply: "_ _ _Wait, there's more, one-day last week, I overheard my mother telling her best friend – while she was on the phone. How she had hired the service of a therapist! To make love to her!" She cried.

I interrupt Say-Say: "Wait – a – minutes how do this therapist's – lover look?" I ask.

Say-Say snap – saying: "_ _ _I only seen him off distant once! He's brown skin and he have an afro!" She reply.

I shouted: "_ _ _Oh – my God! I think I might know who this therapists lovers!" I said.

Say-Say ask: "_ _ _You do!" She ask.

I said: "_ _ _Yes, he just be my roommate. His name is James Crawford! And, he has been bragging about this lady friend! Who has been paying him for sex!", I said.

Shaking her head in dis-belief Say-Say whisper: "_ _ _uh – uh – uh! My Dad's will kill him!" She whisper.

_____After a brief pause I ask: "_ _ _Honey, could I get you a strewberry slush or something?", I ask

Say-Say reply: "_ _ _No Honey, It's too early in the morning for that shit!" She said.

I frowned and reply: "_ _ _Oh excuse me!"

Say-Say came back – saying: "_ _ _But, if you really want to get me something; you can get _ _ _!"

Frowning, I reply; "_ _ _Sarah! It's too early in the morning for f_ _ _ _ _g!" I said.

Smiling, she jokenly said: "_ _ _Chicken – chicken! But could we get together later for a movie!" She said, before driving away.

____CHAPTER – THREE____

Narrators: Tootie Emerge from kneel-ing upon the bedside after her pimp – boy friends had just given her a marijuana – shot gun! Exhaling heavily, she snap – saying: "_ _ _That's – it, that's my last hit! – I am gona get some help!", she shouted.

_____Tootie, A twenty years old mother of five. Had lived in blk. bottom neighborhood. Her entire life. Tootie was the produce of a woman; who had been gang – rape!

Tootie's mother's, A career drug addict herself. Had raised tootie entirely – up, on government programs. such as food – stamps and welfare_ _ _

Tootie had no schooling. In fact, she had never been out of the compound of this neighborhood. At twenty, Tootie was pregnant with her sixth child. And If ask, she couldn't tell you the names of the father's! of any of her childrens.

Although Tootie had no schooling, she couldn't read, reading! And she couldn't write, writing! _ _ _She was street – smart! Today, Tootie had made a decision! While sitting on the toilet.

That, she was no longer gona play – Russians – roulette with her life _ _ _ having baby – after baby and dealing in drugs.

She cited: "_ _ _I am gona make something ou my life! – Even if it's killed me!" she mumble.

_____Today, Tootie had ask her pimp – boyfriend. To take her to this rehabilitation – work – shop. That was sponsor by the N.A.A.C.P. she had heard about on the local radio station.

Tootie's knew, she couldn't fix what's broken inside. Until she break tides with her drugs habit. Just then, A loud voicand – like explosion erupted! It had the equilibrium of an earthquake. Tootie whisper: "_ _ _I think my lord is trying to tell me something!"

Fast – forward.

After the initial introduction while, inside this encamp – group this therapist's – doctor's prompt Tootie to render her welcome – introduction first: "_ _ _My name is Tootie!" She pause for a lost of words. "_ _ _Twenty years I've been lock within the compound of my home! But, this morning, glory – be – to God!! I looks into my bath – room mirror! And saw something inside of me! I – did – not – like!"

(She pause again before saying) If the truth – be – told! It was after I had let my pimp – boy friend give me a marijuana – shot – gun! – It hit me, like – a tons – of bricks! A voice echo. '_ _ _Tootie – Tottie! My long lost child! come out from that darkness!'

(She pause again then say). So I got – up! came here today, to tell somebody! That every-body is somebody special! In sight of God! – If you'll would excuse me – a minute! I think I am gona shout!!____

_____While Tootie was confessing. I was at the library; attempting to complete a essay – term paper. Knowing all too well; I couldn't afford to fail this course. Slowly, I mimic copying word – for word; from this book: '_ _ _Temperature measured on a scale based on absolute – zero. As layman, the theory on absolute – zero and its in house speed at which it moved. Put in place the 3rd law of thermodynances _ _ _'

_____I stopped writing and start pondering my thoughts: '_ _ _No, I couldn't afford to fail this course; and loose my scholar-ship! Knowing that A.T. and T. couldn't give me another grant! Most black college could not complete against thoses white – big – names – colleges! when it came to granting scholarships!'

_ _ _ What I really would like to do; right about now. Is to hook – up with my girl, Say-Say! (Instantly) I start dialing her number:

"_ _ _Sarah – honey! Would you like to go to Caro – wind?" I ask.

Say-Say snap – saying: "_ _ _Tim, I would love to go! But I don't have anything to wear!", She said.

I snap – saying: "_ _ _Honey anything you put on, look good on you!" I said.

Say-Say then reply: "_ _ _Thank you for saying that Tim; Maybe I can find something to put on!"

I then say: "_ _ _O.k., I will pick – you up around 10:15!" I said while hanging up.

Narrators: Caro – wind theme park had been thee place. Many area black colleges students would go at the climax of spring break. I was most appreciative. When my work study supervisor; thought enough of me. And gaved me two free theme park tickets. Plus, authorization to drive the mail van.

_ _ _ I felt, as if I was shitting – in high cotton! One of my Gullah – ancestor's – phrase line.

Minutes later, I arrived at Wal-mart. where I pick-up: '_ _ _One ice chest – 10 lbs. bag of ice – a bag of char-coals – and a miniature grill – Two slice 1 kg of pork chops – 1 small 1kg of drums – sticks – and a package of franks!

I left Wal-mart, at 9:59. speeding I pulled – up at SAY-SAY house, late! She ran out wearing a close fitting pair – of – jean. With a jacket top. That was tied around her neck. Smiling, I greeted her saying: "_ _ _Honey you look great!", I whisper she respond: "_ _ _Thanks! (then ask) Are we gona stay overnight?"

I snap – saying: " _ _ _Girl! Your mothers wouldn't allowed that!", I countered, Say-Say then reply: "_ _ _For your information Tim! – My mother's isn't home! She left the house early this morning!"

Now looking around, the van she ask: "_ _ _How did you pull this off?" She pointed I respond: " _ _ _Oh! After my supervisor gaved me two free tickets! – I ask her about driving the van!"

Say-Say snap – saying: "_ _ _Wait – a – minutes! – Why is this bitch being so nice to you? Is you f_ _ _ _ _g her?" She ask.

Smiling, I said: " _ _ _No honey! – Ain't nothing like that!", I tried to explain. Frowning Say-Say snap: _ _ _It better not be!", she snap – I then ask. "_ _ _Honey do I detect jel-ousy??, I ask.

She dismiss – saying: "_ _ _No – Tim! Ain't nothing like that!" She smiled.

Narrators: After 45 minutes of driving. We exit the interstate on to the Caro – wind free way. And commence driving down that miles – long corridor.

Minutes later, I found a parking space in the D – section. Then, we hurried our way to the front entrance. There, we encounter a long line of tickets – seekers.

Fortunately, having advance tickets. We were permitted to walk right in. Once inside, Say-say literally led me directly to the rides. pointing to the ferris wheel. Say-Say shouted: "_ _ Tim-o-thy, that's what I want to ride first!", She said.

I countered saying: "_ _ _Say-Say! That thing must be five stories high! – Are you sure you want to ride that??", I ask

Pulling onto my arm's she yelled: "_ _ _ Tim! I don't care how high its; I want to ride!", She shouted.

Narrators: After getting into this ferris – wheel – line. We had to wait some 20 minutes. Before we were seated. Row – by – row loading! Until this large wheel; Had to rotate some 50 feets into the air.

Up here, I got a birds eye view! of this theme park landscape. Trembling, I felt a lump moving up my neck. Just before Say-Say start playfully shifting her littler body. Causing ours seat, to shake! I whisper: "_ _ _Stop doing that Say-Say!" Just before the entire ferris wheel began moving.

Say-Say start laughing and yelled: "_ _ _Chicken, chicken! – My man is afraid of a littler ferris wheel!" She yelled.

I shouted: "_ _ _Lord, If you let me get off this ferris wheel –", I felt sick in my stomach. My head was spinning like a top! _ _ _"

Narrators: When we finally got off the ferris wheel. I kneeled – over and kiss the ground and shouted: " _ _ _No more ferris wheel for me!"

Afterwith, Say-Say rode a half dozen rides alone! And while getting off the water log – ride. Say-Say somehow, persuaded me to ride the merry – go – round. Reluctant! Ten minutes later, we exit the merry – go – round; Into a crowd of pedestrians. Walking in all directions.

Say-Say then caught a – hold of my arms and shouted: "_ _ _Tim! – wait – minuters! – I need to catch my breathe _ _ _"

Suddenly un-intentionally the body of a male pedestrians bumped into me. Recognizing James, my room mate. Who yelled: "_ _ _ Oh excuse me my brother! – you didn't tell me you was coming to the park today!" He wasn't alone. Before I could respond. Say-Say shouted: "_ _ -Momaa! What – are you doing here – and who is this man??" I was shock. That was when Say-Say Mother said: "_ _ _Child! – Don't you start with me! (she pause) James just ask me about coming here last night!" James then intervene and ask: "_ _ _So you're the John – Doe! That's dating her daughters!" He ask.

Say-Say mothers interrupt: "_ _ _James here, is my therapist's – friend, that's all!" She tried saying.

Out of frustration Say-Say shouted: "_ _ _Tim! Please get me away from these two!"

Upon walking away. I call out to James: "_ _ _Nigger! I'll get – up with you later! (Turning) facing Say-Say I said. "_ _ _Honey! Don't get so hysterical oversee-ing your mother's with another man! After – all, it couldn't have been a surprise – after you heard what she said to your father's some night ago_ _ _"

Hugging Say-Say now, I whisper: "_ _ _Don't let this ruins ours first day together _ _ _"

Say-Say then reply: "_ _ _Tim! I cain't help it! – (pause) How can she do that?" She whisper.

As we approach the exit – gate I whisper: "_ _ _Say-Say, we cain't leave just yet, we have a cook out date, R-e-m-e-m-b-e-r?" Disregarding my last statement Say-Say snap – saying: "_ _ _See-ing my mothers cheat on my fathers like that hurt like hell!" She echo, still sobbing.

Narrator's _ I hate see-ing Say-Say like this! – Anyway, this was just another black relationship gone bad!

When we finally reach the van. We gathers ours supplies. And re-enter the park through the camp ground entrance. Once inside we found an un-occupied piece of real – estate. Where we spread ours blanket.

There wasn't a cloud, in the sky. What – a – perfect day for a picnic! Carowind was first among theme parks in this area. To be integrated of course, you couldn't detect that today. For all the predominate surrounding white camper's; In this park today.

Shortly after firing – up the grill. Wait-ing for the coal to get hot. Before putting the meats on. Say-Say and I laid there on the blanket. Talking, Say-Say whisper: "_ _ _Why, why? – would a woman do that to her husband?" She sobbed. I whisper: "_ _ _That's a good question honey!"

Say-Say then reply: "_ _ _And my fathers, really – really love that woman!" She cry out!

I said: "_ _ _Apparently honey! She don't love him; like he love her!" I whisper.

Say-Say sit – up and whisper: "_ _ _Of all the dirty things, my mothers have done _ _ _!" I rubbed her arm and whisper. "_ _ _Honey – honey! Settle down, everything she's doing now. Will eventually come out in the washs!" I said.

Say-Say then mumble: "_ _ _I hope like hell, it does!" She mumble crying un-controllable, I reach over, wiping tears from her eyes. I whisper: "_ _ _Honey, this is the first time. I had, the pleasure of laying – up with you! (pause) on a blanket!", I smiled.

Smiling now, Say-Say snap – saying: "_ _ _Nigger – please! out here, on a blanket, in the open! _ Be – for – real!" She laughs.

I reply: "_ _ _You know, you're much – more beautiful! When you're happy – laughing!" I whisper.

Say-Say then reply: "_ _ _Why thank – you Tim!" She snap and voiced. "_ _ _Something is burning! I jumped up. Moving toward the open flame on the grill. I yelled: "_ _ _Ours meat is on fir-er!". I yelled

Say-Say asked: "_ _ _Is it's all ruin?", She ask.

Frowning, I whisper: _ _ _Let's just stay, there won't be an any rare chops today!" I said.

Say-Say whisper: "_ _ _That's not a problem; who eat pork – chops are rare anyway?" She implies.

Shaking my head in agreement, I said: _ _ _Honey, you're alright in my book." I said: _ _ _While removing the burns meats from the grill _ _ _

_ _ _ _ _ _ _ _By 5:10, we were pack and enroute back home. While driving Say-Say whisper: _ _ _Tim, today has been fun! I cain't remember when I had more fun! – Thank you for inviting me!" She said. While steering into the fast lane I whisper: _ _ _Thank you for coming! (pause) Hey! Isn't that your mother's car up ahead?" I ask Say-Say snap – saying. "_ _ _Yes! And she got that Crawford man; driving my Daddy's car!

I reply: "_ _ _Gee-e, they're moving pretty – fast!", I shouted. Say-say then shouted. "_ _ _Tim, catch – up with them; and run – up in their rear." She shouted.

I snap – saying: "_ _ _Say-Say! Do you want me to go to jail?", I ask. Say-Say then reply. "_ _ _ No Tim!" She cryed. "_ _ _I hate see-ing what she's doing to my Dads!"

_ _ _ _ _ _ _ _ _Within minutes, they were out of sight. Fifteen minutes later we got off on the Greensboro exit. And drove seven miles. Where we pulled up in front of Say-Say house. There, I notice Say-Say father's car parked in the driveway. Getting out she smack me on the cheek and whisper: "_ _ _Will you call me later please!" she whisper.

I then reply: "I will, I promise!" While driving away_ _ _

After dropping off the van I took that short walk to my dorm's room. Inside, James my room-mate was in the shower sing-ing away.

I switch the remote of my small television set on the 6:00 news: "_ _ _This is the N.B.C six – o – clock news! – Today, the directors of the F.B.I – Mister Hoover made the following remarks – about the civil rights movement_ _ _ 'In my views! I think theses negros are moving too fast! – They should wait for ours justice system to evolve! – And stop some of theses protect – demonstrations_ _ _!

Immediately after Mr. Hoover's remark's. This broadcasters announcer said: "_ _ _Over in our nation capitol today. A Washington – post reporter's interviews doctor kings – who had this to say – 'in respond to Mr. Hoover's remark. Doctor Kings comment: "_ _ _Black folkes don't have time to wait any longer for freedoms! – Beside, we have been waiting 100 years to long _ _ _"

Coming out of the shower. James appeared – spooked! See-ing me, he ask: "_ _ _Did you have fun today?", He ask. I answer and said. "_ _ _Hell yes! Any time I am with my lady – I always have a good time_ _ _"

Walking just inches from where I was standing. James Whisper: "_ _ _Man, you ought to be ar–shame of yourself! That girl is only 13 yrs. old!" he whispers.

I snap and yelled: "_ _ _For your information, she won't be 13 until next month! But she's a hell – of – a lot morer mature then any 20 yrs. old woman, I know!" I shouted. James then ask: "_ _ _Have you f_ _ k her yet?" He ask. I shouted back. "_ _ _That ain't none of your f_ _ _ _ _ g business!"

Frowning James reply: "_ _ _It may not be my business! – But it could be the police – business! – When they come and pick your black ass up for rape!"

Frowning myself, I yelled: "_ _ _What, in the hell, are you talking about nigger?? I ask.

Pointing his finger James mocked: "_ _ _Your best chance, is that littler bitch don't go home; and start running off at the mouths to her fathers _ _ _"

I reply: "_ _ _Why!!", I ask. James then whisper: "_ _ _Because if she say anything to her fathers – about today her mothers is going straight to the police! And have your black ass charge with statutory – rape!" He whisper.

Shaking my head in dis be-belief I said: "_ _ _Ain't that some shit! This woman is gona black – mail her owns daughters!

Narrators__ Just then, my cellphone sounded. It was Say-Say, her voice sound extremely loud; and she was talking fast: "_ _ _Hello – honey! (she started) you know as soon as I got in the house! – My mother's start fussing and threaten-ning me!!

_ _ _Saying, if I say anything to my Dad's – when he come home; About what happen today! – She's going straight to the police! – And press charges on you for rape!!__

I had Say-Say on my speaker's – phone James, who was standing nearby; was laughing his ass off! Say-Say was talking so fast. I interrupte and said: "_ _ _And, she had the nerves to ask you; How many times we had sex!" Say-Say never stop talking. Before I interrupte her again and said.

"_ _ _Honey – honey! Slow down, we don't have anything to worry about! The lord is my witness! Cause I haven't ever touchs you!_ _ _

Say-Say then said: "_ _ _I know that Tim! – I wish you had! – (pause) Just to think, she would stupe so low!" she ended.

I then said: "_ _ _Right now, your mother is running scared! She will do anything to keep the heat off her ass_ _ _" I whisper.

There was a brief silent before Say-Say whisper: "_ _ _ I wasn't going to up-set my father's; In the first place with her mess!" She said.

I then reply: "_ _ _That's terrific! Because your mother's littler therapists – friend over here! Been itchings with anticipation of getting me arrested!" I said loud enough so James could hear.

Say-Say then reply: "_ _ _Honey, I will testify if I has to; And tell the world! You never touchs me! – Although, I wish you had _ _ _"

Smiling, I end ours call in saying: "_ _ _Honey, don't worry about a thing! – This whole thing will soon blow over!"

Narrators __ The following morning while walking to class. I notice that traffic on campus; seem a bit more conjectives over in front of the administrations building. I saw a crews of media – peoples. Busy finishing setting up. What appear to be a interview – platform.

As I made my way across the front – lawns. I heard this white commentator's voiced – out his opening introduction: "_ _ _ Today, this is a special addition to news – break! – I am here with the sport person for A.T. and T. college!

"_ _ _To get some answers – for all theses protest – demonstrations! (he smiled)

Turning, he said. "_ _ _Miss lady! – Because of all theses protest – demonstrations in this area! – The K.K.K. membership have risen by 100,000! – Do you have a respond?", He ask.

While moving a pair of glasses. This lady sport – person reply: "_ _ _Yess – sir! It just goes to show; That thoses whites boys! Have been itchings for a reason to enlist more members!" She reply.

This commentator's face change color around his nose. To a redish – orange! Before he snap: "_ _ _Miss lady are you trying to say. That this institution advocate all theses demonstrations! – I'll – regardless of the klans increase membership!" he said.

While putting her glasses back on she snap: "_ _ _Look Mister! You know as well as I! That A.T. and T. is a state's own's institution! – we don't advocate breaking any laws! (pause)

_ _ _Yet, if any laws were broken! Its Jim – Crows – laws!!" She snap.

Smiling this commentators yelled, "_ _ _Just what I thought! – You people do support theses civil – rights – demonstrations!", He shouted.

Frowning, she said: "_ _ _This inter-view is over!!" Now walking away.

Narrators__ After that interview, the demonstrations intensify all across the south, at A.T. and T. by mid afternoon 75% of students walked out of classes. In support of the demonstrations.

Greensboro city policemen went on high – alert. They began targeting and killing young blk. men! Today, the local papers printed a headline: "_ _ _Three blacks panthers arrested for mass – killings!"

This predominate white police forced; under – handerly took racial profiling to the next level! On a mission, to eradicate the negros race!

__ _Jim Crows Laws were the measuring – stick by which theses by which theses policemen governs!

Narrators__ Today, Say-Say and her 16 yrs old brother were enroute to school.

They were pulled over at a traffic light. By two white policemen.

Jumping out of their squad – car. The first cop yelled: "_ _ _Boy, turn your car off! – And put your hands up on the steering wheel!", he shouted.

Littler – boy joyner's yelled. While attempting to get his I.D. – from the glove compartment: "_ _ _officers! – Why are you stopping me?" Joyner echo. The second cop yelled – out while coming up on the passenger's side of the car.

"_ _ _Watch out!! – He's going for his gun!", He yelled.

Suddenly, both cops commense firing two shots each! Instantly, Littler – boy Joynes body slumped – over the steering wheel life-less! – Say-Say screamed: "_ _ _You'll shot my brother! – For noth–ing!" She cryed. The second cop jerk the door open and shouted.

"_ _ _Shut – up – gal! – This boy was reaching for his gun!"

Say-Say shouted: "_ _ _Liars! My brother don't own a gun!"

Narrators__ Say-Say was so shaken by her brother – killing. She had to be transport by ambulance. To the psycho ward for observation.

Alternately, this killing, was the fourth black man killed. By these two cops. Within the last 30 days! There were a large public outcry. Behind the last killing! The entire black neighborhood demonstrated police headquarters.

Eventually, both cops were finally arrested. Later, theirs killings were up-grade as a federal – hate crime. Nonetheless, after six months of litigation. Both cops were sentence 45 days each; and fired!

_____A slap on the wrist! For taking a human life!

At the trial, after the jurors had handed down, theirs judgement. Say-Say screamed out loud in the court room: "_ _ _Do a black man life's matter around here! – It seem like blk. people lifes is not worst a plug – nickel! – To, you whites folkes!" She yelled.

Narrators__ Mrs. Joyner request a private funeral for her son. There were less then 20 person in attendance.

Say-Say took her brother death extremely hard. It triggered an emotional – disorder of nympholepsy! That left a lasting – effect of bitterness; Toward all policemen. Yet, despite all these feeling. Mrs. Joyner's choose Say-Say to deliver the final remark; for her brother.

Standing there, at the grave site. Say-Say citied: "_ _ _There will be no eulogy for John Henry Joyner Jr. today! – (she pause) _ _ _I know that the lord giveth! – And the lord taketh away! Bless be the name of the lord!"

She stop and looked over at her mother before saying. "_ _ _Momma I know you told me not to talk so long! Or to say anything about littler Joyner's killing!

She pause again before mumbling! "_ _ _But, they didn't had to kill my brother like they did! They shot him, like they were shooting a dog! In the street! (sobbling)_ _ _ For no reason other – then, he was black! _ _ _"

Say-Say spoked for twelve and a half minutes. Before ending: "_ _ _John Henry Joyner Jr!"

She voiced now looking up! – "You will never be for-gotten! – Nor will we ever forgive these two whites cops! – Who took you from us too soon! _

There wasn't a dry pair of eyes standing around that day. Two days after the funeral. Say-Say went back to school under a racial – tension – environment! That best could be describe as a ticking time bomb! And, on her first day back; There was a bomb – scare!

Narrators_ When I first got the alarm. I rushs up to Say-Say school. Where I saw her and a group of students; running out of the south side gate. When she saw me, she ran and jump into my arms. And yelled: "_ _ _Tim! you must've heard about the bomb – scare! (pause) Them cracker's are threat-ening violence again! she yelled.

I snap – saying: "_ _ _Are you O.K?" I ask. She reply: "_ _ _ I am fine! can we go have lunch? – I am hungry – as – hell!" I smiled and say: "_ _ _Sound good to me! – What about the waffle house? I pointed across the street.

She reply: "_ _ _That's o.k. with me! _ _ _?

Inside the waffle house I order: "_ _ _One ham and cheese sandwithces on toast, slice!"

Say-Say whisper: "_ _ _Oh, and one large coke, easy on the ice! With two straws!" Say-Say whisper.

Just then the juke box start playing the song, Teacher's – pet': '_ _ _I – want – to – be the teacher's pet! – I want to be huddle and cuddle _ _ _'

Facing me at the table , Say-Say whisper: "_ _ _I would rather be Tim-o-thy – pet!"

Leaning across the table she kiss me on the tip of my nose. Before she ask: "_ _ _When a man love a woman, like you say you do! would it be fair to say! That man should want to make love to that wo-man!", She ask.

I answer; "_ _ _Of course that man should want to make love! to his woman." I whisper

She lean across the table agan and held – up her parse. And whisper: "_ _ _Great, look I've $46.25 all the money; I have in the world! Lets take this money and catch the next bus. And get a motel room. For a couple of hours!

Hesitantly, I reply: "_ _ _Sound great!", I whisper. Rushing Say-say start putting our order into a to – go bag. She then ask. "_ _ _Tim, what are you waiting on?"

Smiling , I jokingly said: "_ _ _The bus!"

_____Twenty minutes later, Say-Say and I got off the bus. In front of the red – roof – inn. She suggest I go ahead and get the room. While she remain at the bus – stop. As a pre – cautionary – measure.

It took just 20 minutes to register for the room. Being,, that the transaction was paid for in cash. Coming out of the motel office. I signal Say-Say, to come across the street. When she reach me, I gaved her the magnetic – key and said: "_ _ _Honey! we're in room 4625!", I whisper she said. "This got to my lucky – day! Because 46.25 was all the money I had in the world!" She whisper agan.

I then made her a promise: "_ _ _Say-Say! Don't make it sound so bad honey! I will pay you back!" I said.

_____ We wasn't in the room three minutes before Say-Say boldly start stripping within seconds, she was completely nude. Her littler body picture an image of sweet chocolate!

I stood there spellbound. Suddenly she called out, breaking the silent: "_ _ _Timothy! What are wait-ing on? – Get your cloths off!" She whisper.

I completely freaked out! Moving away, I whisper: "_ _ _Say-Say, I cain't do this to you! I want it to be perfect and legal! We do make love_ _ _!

When I said that. It was like I had bitten off the head of a rattle – snake. Shew was boiling with angle! I since that she was too emotional up-set right then.

"_ _ _Tim-o-thy!– You cain't do this to me! – My body is on firer! – Please, don't make me beg!!" She mourn.

I tried un-successfully to reason with Say-Say; with no avail, before she abruptly put her cloths back on. And yelled: "_ _ _Got – damned, take me home!", She shouted. Twenty minutes later. We were back on the bus. In route to her house. When the bus arrives at her stop. She got off without saying goodbye!

Narrators__ Colored – People the story continue. Attorney form N.A.A.C.P. and the local branch of black – news network. Had teams up, in an under – cover operation. To investigate the dozen of black men. Whom had been killed or accuse!

Solely on the accusation, on one red – neck white woman a miss Kitty's Washington. According to reports. Miss – Washington had conspired a scheme coming straight from the pages of Jim Crows – Laws books.

Twelve times, Miss Washington made sworn – accusation against Negros men of her being rape! And on her word alone! Determine to be judge, juror and executioner's! Case number – one: _ _ _Miss Washington claim she had been rape. In an elevator by a 275 lbs black man – according to police reports Miss Washington said. 'She was overpower by a very monster – looking colored man!'

_ _ _Ours intelligent report indicate this 275 lbs man – whom name, 'Honey boy' was gay.

_ _ _Anywhere Miss Kittys had Mr. Honey boy arrested. While on my way to jail. Mr. Honey boy was murder by 2 policemen_ _ _

Case number two: _ _ _Miss Washington claims she was rape. In her words by this colored bus – boy. At this restaurant where she work! – severals whites employees killed this bus – boy before the police arrived_ _ _

Case number three: Miss Washington claims she was rape by two Negros men. Whom she had known from her work place. Records shown that both men were in Jail; at the time she claims she was rape! – weeks later, both men were somehow killed by cause – un-known! _ _ _

The teams of prosecutors – attorneys corroborate and found fowl – play; On each of the 12 cases. Miss Kittys was later prosecuted and sanction. One-year probation.

After Miss Kittys was found guilty. And, by public demand, Chief Portee was asked to step down. For his involvement; Linking him the real master–mind. Behind all these murdering schemes.

Looking back, private – first – class, Portee got his big break. To become chief. When he was hired by mayor John Blatts. While he was back in the police – academy. For his out-standing display. Which dis-tinquish him-self as a segregationer's advoctor's.

When private Portee first became chief he made a sweeping change; In the overall structure of the police department. Chief Portee first master-mind, a way to furlough. Those two blk. cops. He then waves the used of body camera! And dis-continue keeping record on his fellow officer's. For all theirs drive by shootings!

In addition, Chief Portee had secretly organized a white – lifes – matter coalition. To combat theirs counter rivalry.' The blacks – lifes matter – group.

Today, the N.A.A.C.P were demonstrating outside police headquarter. In retaliation to all the police – killings of blk. men. Looking, their signs said it all: '_ _ _Blacks – lifes – matter! _ _ _Black have rights too! _ _ _Enough is enough!'

Narrators__ as the demonstrators paraded back and forth! They became more intense and grow – stronger in rebellions!

Directly in front of police headquarter's. Standing along the steps. A well organize group of whites – skin heads! paraded along the steps! As they march displaying their signs: '_ _ _Littler black sam bo! – Go back to Africa! – The only good nigger, is a dead nigger!'

They suddenly, began sing-ing: '_ _ _Two – four – six – eight! – we don't want to integrate! – Two – four – six – eight!! – we don't want to I–N–T–E–G–R–A–T–E_ _ _!!!'

While they sing, this Negro leaders began addressing the crowd: "_ _ _Black folkes can no longer stand on the side line! – while ours brothers are shot down in the streets like dogs!

_ _ _We can no longer stand by and do nothing! while ours brothers are trapped with false accusations of rape! And later they're killed or sentences to life in jail!

_ _ _And we damned cain't wait for white justice to evolve!

_ _ _We can no longer turn thee other cheek! – And allowed the whiter man – to slap us on the other! This speaker pause before saying.

"_ _ _My bros and my sisters! – The N.A.A.C.P solicit your help! – To fight against these Jim Crows – giant! – xxxx we will fight this giant in the voting polls! – If we don't win there!

xxxx We will fight this giant court room! – If we don't get justice there! xxxx We will fight this giant right here – on the streets of Greensboro!!"

Looking now across the street at the group of skin – heads this black speaker shouted: "_ _ _And, to my pale – skins bros – across the street!! There won't be any peace! – until we all are free_ _ _"

Narrators___ While this brother was speaking. I cross main street under the watchful eyes of severals policemen. And slowly start walking along the sidewalk toward campus.

Once inside campus instead of going to my dorms – room. I made a pit – stop and pick up the mail – van. From there, I rushs over to Say-Say. Being I haven't heard from her; since that disappointing encounter. Back at the motel.

A short time later, I arrived at Say-Say house. As I pulled up into her drive way. Like always, I saw her coming out from under her garage. When she approach me I quickly said: "_ _ _Honey! We has to talk!" I then motion for her to get in. Surprisingly, without responding, she jump in, leaving the door open.

I snap – saying: "_ _ _ Say-Say! About what happen last week! – I was wrong; would you forgive me?", I ask.

She didn't say a word. She start kissing me passionately! It was then, I heard a voice. From outside the van: "_ _ _Bitch! Get away from my man!" This voice belong to Say-Say. Confuse, I jump pushing this female impersonator's away.

I then shouted; "_ _ _Wait – a – minute! If that's Say-Say out there! (I pointed) Who! in – the – hell, is you??"

By that time, Say-Say walked up to the side of the van and shouted: "Tim! I see you've met this bitch! She is my twin sister!" Say-Say screamed. Now reaching, Say-Say snatch her sister by the collar pulling her out of the van.

I snap – saying: "_ _ _Jesus – Christ! Say-Say, you never told me, you had a twin sister!!" I yelled.

Now, getting in the van Say-Say snap: "_ _ _Tim! You never asked."Say-Say whisper.

I reply: "_ _ _Say-Say honey! I didn't know. I thought I was kissing you!" I said.

Say-Say then whisper: "_ _ _My bad Tim! I should have told you!" She whisper. While placing her head onto my shoulder's. She change the subject – saying.

"_ _ _Now, about what happen back at the motel! Maybe, I was a littler harsh on you! – I am sorry! _ _ _"

Smiling, I ask: _ _ _Then we are good?", I ask. She reply: "_ _ _Yes honey, we're good!" I then ask: "_ _ _Say-Say! – Tell me about this twin sister?" I ask.

Frowning, Say-Say whisper. "_ _ _There ain't much to tell; except she just got of the reformatory! – For stabbing a girl in the eye with a pencil." She snap.

I shouted: "_ _ _A pencil?" I mimic her.

Say-Say added: "_ _ _Yea, something that happen, when were in the 4th grade!" _ _ _

I whisper: "_ _ _This twin sister of your is rough!" _ _ _

Say-Say reply: "_ _ _Even back then, the heifer's and I couldn't get alone! (pause) Oh, and I don't want you near her ever again!" Sher warns.

I whisper: "_ _ _I won't honey!" I promise."

Say-Say the collard me and warns: "_ _ _Nigger! – Now kiss me like you was kissing that bitch!" Instantly, our lips me passionately for several minutes before I push her away and echo.

"_ _ _Now that we've made – up! Maybe, I can go and get some sleep!" Now, putting the van in reverse and driving off_ _ _

_____After the assembly. Much of what this school president had said. Fell on deaf – ears! Shortly thereafter, 95% of those students; went out and participated in demonstrating right there on campus.

And, those two students leader's. Whom previously had been expelled. Were over in front of campus headquarter's. Being interviews on a live television network. Hosted by a commentator's; from the meet the – press show.

All this, in front of huges audience of students! Standing – witnessing this commentator's opening statement: "_ _ _Today I am here at A.T. and T. college! with two of it's students activates! who led yesterday big – marchs!"

Narrators: The next day, the Washington post newspaper. Ran a front page headline.

On the president sending 12,000 national guard men to Mississippi – state – college. To help maintain order.

As a back – lash, hundreds of black college students all across the south. Took to the streets, demonstratings!

Meanwhile, A.T and T. president called a special assembly – meeting. His opening statement: "_ _ _Good evening! I call this assembly today! To reflex on all the civil – rights demonstrations! We been having around the south! And other black colleges!

_ _ _I want to make it un-mistakably – clear! That A.T. and T. college will not tolerate, having ours campus destroy! During these demonstrations!

_ _ _As your school president, my number – one concerns. Is to keep the doors of this institution free from devastation!_ _ _"

_____After the assembly, much of what this school president had said. Fell on deaf – ears! Shortly thereafter, 95% of those students; went out and participated in demonstrating right there on campus.

And those two students leader's. whom previously had been expelled. were over in front of campus headquarter's. Being interviews on a live television network. Hosted by a commentator's; from the meet the – press show.

All this, in front of huges audience of students! standing – witnessing this commentator's opening statement: "_ _ _Today I am here at A.T. and T. college! with two of it's students activates! Who led yesterday big – marchs!"

Holding the microphone with a firm grip. This commentators ask: "_ _ _would one – of you boys! Tell me why you people! Are making so much fuss over segregation – policies! That had been the law – of the land! Every since you – people got here?" He shouted.

This 1st student reply: "_ _ _Because – Sir! Enough is – Enough!" He reply.

The 2nd student interrupt: " _ _ _Sir, we're tired of having you – people! (he pointed) piss all over us; And turn around and tell us, its rain-ing!!" He shouted.

The 1st student shouted: "_ _ _We want the same rights and privileges you have! – speaking on behalf of our students – body! We believe by participating in this demonstration! _ _ _Is ours way we show ours support_ _ _"

_____Both student stormed off the scene. Just seconds – before the entire staging area came under heavy firer! By a machine gun like sound; resemblings an A-K-47!

Just then, I saw this commentator's head shattered! A jet stream – of blood! Vaporize into the air. Crawling, for dear life! 50 feets away, I emerge – up out of a man – hole!

Just then, my cellphone ring! It was Say-Say, she sound upset: "_
_ _Tim, meet me at E.M.S hospital! My Momma been shot!" She
sound out – of breathe.

_____I rushs to the hospital; running most of the way.
Twenty minutes later, I walk into the lobby. And found Say-Say,
pacing back – and forth. Near the entrance of the waiting room.
When I approach her I asked.

"_ _ _Say-Say! How is your mother?, I ask.

Say-Say then said" Tim, you're all bloody! What happen to you?"
She ask.

I snap saying "_ _ _That's a long story! (pause) How is your
mother?" I ask again.

She finally whisper: "_ _ _I don't know they won't tell me anything!
Other then, she's undergoing surgery" Say-Say whisper.

Sadie was standing near, interrupted "_ _ _Sarah, I just overheard
2 doctors coming out of the operation room commenting 'what – a
– tragedy! Now there's one killed and another, critical – wounded!"

Say-Say nervously mumble: "_ _ _Oh Lord – Jesus!" She mumble.

I put my arms around her and whisper: "_ _ _Say-Say that doctor
could have been talking about someone else!" I whisper.

_____About that time another doctor came out of operation.
And call out: "_ _ _Who is next of kin; for Sarah Joyners?" he ask.

Say-Say nervously moved forward and Say: "_ _ _That would be
us! – Is my mother alright?" She ask.

This doctor said: "_ _ _Your mothers came out of surgery,
satisfactory! un-fortunately, I am afraid she will be paralyze from
her waist down!" While walking away, this doctor turn around and

said. "_ _ _Oh she had been consistently – asking for someone name John Henry!" He walk away.

Sadie frowned and say: "_ _ _She can call all she want! But Dad's ain't coming!" Sadie whisper

Say-Say interrupted her: "_ _ _Sadie – Mae shut – the – hell – up!" Turning she ask the doctor. "_ _ _Can we see her?" Say-Say ask.

This doctor reply: "_ _ _As soon as the nurses get her all clean – up; And move to a room!' he said.

_____Forty – five minutes later we went up to mother Joyner room. And found her laying on her back. Her eyes were closed, tho, she wasn't ar – sleep as soon as we walked in, she start – mumbling: "_ _ John – Henry – John – Henry! I am so sorry! Will you forgive me!!" She mumble.

Sadie reach over and touch her and reply: "_ _ _Momma, daddy isn't here; who shot you?"

Sadie ask Mrs. Joyner's hesitated before answering "_ _It was a jealous ass wife! That shot me!" Mrs. Joyners shouted.

Sadie said: "_ _ _Momma, that jealous – ass wife! Got you good!" Sadie snap.

Mrs. Joyners open her eyes and reply: "_ _ _That's alright, I will one day have the last laughs!"

_____Just then, the nurse came back in the room and reply: "_ _ _Sorry folkes, your time is up! This poor woman need to rest"

Sadie then countered: "_ _ _Miss nurse! This woman need more then rest, (pointing) Her ass need a prayer!"

Say-Say reply: "_ _ _Sadie, must you always be so rogue_ _ _!"

_____Minutes later, we walked out of the hospital. Now in the car Say-Say reply: "_ _ _Tim! I'll drop you off at your dorms!"

Sadie snap – saying: "_ _ _Good! He can sit back in the rear with me!"

Say-Say shouted: "I am not gona tell you anymore; bitch, leave my man alone!!"

Sadie snap – saying: "_ _ _Child, go ahead and drive! – I am not mess-ing with your man!!"

Just then, the local radio – station was broad-casting, news – break: "_ _ _This is news break! – Today one man was killed. And one woman was critical wounded! At a local motel – In what authority believe was a domestic – violence shoot – out!" Say-Say yelled: "_ _ _List-en! This is about Momma_ _ _!"

After a brief pause. Sadie reply: "_ _ _Yes, I heard the rumors, that momma been f_ _ _ _ _ g that man for years!"

Say-Say then reply: "_ _ _That explains why Dad's didn't want to come to the hospital!"

Sadie snap – saying: "_ _ _I don't blame Daddy, I wouldn't go and look my mate in the face knowing she had been caught f_ _ _ _ _ g another man!

Say-Say then reply; "_ _ _Humph – humph! Momma is in trouble!!"

Sadie then reply: "_ _ _I've a feeling Dad's gona leave her black ass!!"

Say-Say whisper: "_ _ _Poor – Momma!"

Sadie frowned and reply: "_ _ _I don't feel sorry for her. Momma knew just what she was doing was wrong_ _ _!"

Narrators: When they reached the house. They found Mister – Henry sitting near the front window, gazing out. Say-Say spoked first: "_ _ _Dad! Momma been shot! she's at the hospital and she have been asking for you!"

Looking straight – forward Mister Henry reply: "_ _ _Child, your mother's will be alright!" Speaking in a non-chalance manner.

Agan Say-Say tried to explain: "_ _ _But Dad, you don't understand! – Momma is paralyze from her waist down (sobbing now) – she cain't walk no more!!"

Mister Henry seem un-moved agan reply: "_ _ _Like I said child! she would be alright!_ _ _Now give me my car key!"

Sadie began shouting: "_ _ _Hur-rah – hur-ah! For dad, it about time you stand – up; and start wearing the pant's in this family!!"

Say-Say then whisper: "Daddy, please don't do anything, pre-mature just yet!!!"

_____Speaking now, out of character. Mr. Henry whisper: "_ _ _Baby girl, a man got – to – do! – What a – man – got – to do!"

Say-Say whisper: "_ _ _Oh God! I think Momma is in trou-ble!!"

_____Mister Henry echo those words while walking out the door.

____CHAPTER FOUR____

After Say-Say drop me off. I notice every where around campus now resemble a war zone. There was miles of yellow – Police, do not cross ticket – tape. Plastered up around the administration building.

Dozens of F.B.I agents were combing the crash – site. For physical evidence. Cautiously, I cross over in front of headquarters. And slowly made my way to my dorm's room.

When I arrived, James was lying on his back. Gazing up, into the ceiling. He spoked first: "_ _ _I heard there were some excitement with your fiancee – family today!" He whisper.

I hesitated before saying: "_ _ _Nothing worst talking to you about!", I snap.

James sit – up and shouted: "Come on Tim! – Are you still sore at me; thinking that I pushed that woman – up! – To go to the police?"

I stop mid ways the floor and yelled – out his name: "_ _ _James – Crawford!! – I don't want to talk to you about it!", I yelled.

James the mumble: "_ _ _O.k! I can dig that!"

Just then my cell phone sounded. It was Say-Say agan. This time, she was calling to tell me about this civil rights leaders; That was shot! While getting off the phone I mumble: "_ _ _When will all the killings stop!" I said out loud.

James, who heard me, reply: "_ _ _When people stop living!" I then said. "But why do these whites people hate us so?, I ask.

James answer: "_ _ _Because, I believe each time most whites see us! – They see a littler bit of themselves in us!" James whisper.

I whisper: "_ _ _That's sick! (pause) Do you think, they will see us any way other than being second class citizen?", I ask.

James laugh and said: "_ _ _Not in this lifetime!!"

Suddenly, two F.B.I agents bogart their way into our room.

"_ _ _Which one of you – boys; is James Crawford?"

This first agent ask. James hesitantly answer. "_ _ _I am James Crawford! Who in the hell want to know?"

The first agent snap: "_ _ _Boy! – I ask the question! – (pause) Is it true you made a comment some days ago!" He stop and began reading from a notepad: "_ _ _Black folkes have rights to bare arms! – I urge you'll to go and grab guns! – Because, white – folkes have theirs!!"

This agent end reading. James reply: "_ _ _Ar – yes I said that last week – while addressing a group of demonstrators!

This second agent then ask: "_ _ _Well boy, where was you on yesterday about this time?"

Before James was able to answer. The other agent shouted: "_ _ _You littler shit-stick! – you took your A-K-47 and brutally kill all them people yesterday!"

James stood up and say: "_ _ _On yesterday, I was down in the audience as a spectators. On this outside meet – the – press show! Down in front of our campus building!_ _ _"

The first agent step forward now placing hand – cuffs on Crawford shouted: "_ _ _Boy! You might have been down yesterday! – But not as a spectators! – I believe you're our's shooters!_ _ _"

This second agent add: "_ _ _Unti then, you're under – arrest!

James said: "_ _ _I am not saying another word; until I talk to my attorney!" James whisper.

While escorting James off. The first agent whisper: "_ _ _That, just might be your best bet boy!_ _ _"

Narrators_____ Just after my 4th period class, Say-Say was park out front of C – hall – building. I greet her saying: "_ _ _Good – evening – beautiful! – ". While getting in her car – she respond: "_ _ _Hi yourself!"

I asked: "_ _ _What's the latest news on your mother?" She answer, "_ _ _I dont know; I haven't talk to her since yesterday!"

I then asked: "_ _ _What – ar-bout your father's?" – She snap saying: "_ _ _Tim! My father's been acting very strange here lately and, I heard him talking on the phone – inquiring about an apartment!", She whisper.

I then said: "_ _ _Say-Say! – Do you really think your father's would leave your mother's", I ask. Say-Say then said: "_ _ _I don't know its hard to tell what my father's would do! – (pause) – He has been a man! – with few words!"

Moving now, pass the hospital entrance – way. I shouted: "_ _ _ Say-Say! – you're passing the hospital!" – She reply: "_ _ _Oh no, they moved her into the annex – building next door.

After parking in the annex parking lot. We went directly to Mrs. Henry room. Once inside, Mrs. Henry ask: "_ _ _Child! – Where is John Henry?" She ask. Say-Say reply: "_ _ _Momma, I hate to tell you this! – But, Dad don't want to see you right now!!"

Mrs. Henry then cry – out: "_ _ _He got to see me child! – I need to tell him, I am sorry!"

She whisper_ _ _

Say-Say then said: "_ _ _Momma, you should know Dad by now! – once he makes–up his mind, thats it_ _ _"

————————————————————Crying now, Mrs. Henry mumble:

"_ _ _ Lord, what am I gona do without John Henry! – I don't have no insurance or income! And, on tomorrow, this hospital gona relief me!!!

She sobbed.

Say – Say whisper; "_ _ _ well Mom, I guess I will be the one to pick you up! – (turning she ask). "_ _ _Tim! – would you come back with me to picks Mom's-up?

I answered: "_ _ _ sure I will!"

Say –Say then whisper: "_ _ _ Momma!

We're not gona stay long! – Dad's been complain-ing about me driving without a license!"

Mrs. Henry reply: "_ _ _ O.K. honey!

Don't forget, the doctor normally makes his rounds about 7:A.M".

Say – say end saying: "_ _ _ stop worrying Momma! – Tim and I will be here around 9: A.M _ _ _".

After leaving the hospital. Say – Say suggest having lunch at Moon – GLO. And promise this time; she will behave!

I said: "_ _ _ Moon – GLO is cool with me!–Anywhere honey! – You're doing the driving _ _ _".

Several minutes later, when we reach the restaurant. Say – Say quickly placed our order: "_ _ _ May we have two mtn. dews – on the rock!". Frowning she add – saying. "_ _ _same old bitch!".

I quickly offered this waitress an apology: "_ _ _Miss! – Please excuse her, she didn't mean that!", I whisper.

Say – Say yelled: "_ _ _ Timothy! Got – damned, stop apologizing to her! – you know she got – the hots – for you _ _ _"

After the waitress left. I said: "_ __ Say – Say! – you should know by now! I only have eyes for you!

Sobbing now, Say – Say said: "_ _ _ Here lately Tim! – I've been experiencing these emotional – feeling! – of don't trust! Any female around you _ _ _" she whisper.

I said: "_ _ _ Say – Say! I am not going anywhere! – I am here, for you, for – ever!", I assure her.

After saying that, Say – Say said:

"_ _ _ Tim! Tell me something about your past?", she ask. She caught me off guard. I cited:

"_ _ _ Honey, there's not much to tell about my past. Except, back when I was 15 yrs old. My mother send me to Rochector N.Y. To live with my father's!

It was back during the winter! – of one of the worst snow fall- for that area. Since the weather – bureau – began keeping records. Anyway, to make a long story short. My father's was killed three months. After I got up there by, a drive – by – shooting!

After his death, this lady land – lord told me. That the rent was paid up for two weeks! – After that, I had to vacate the premises!

_ _ _ Disastrous as it was! – There I was in this big city! With no relative! – And no place to go! – So I took a gamble! And went and pawn my boom – box. And brought myself a shovel! – where I went about the neighborhood! – Soliciting my services shoverling snow – from the local merchants store – front!

_ _ _ I was so successful! – After four days, I had earned almost $ 1,000 dollars! – Having earned so much money. I was afraid that the neighborhood – houdlum's would rob me! – So I secretly took a pillar case and made myself a money belt!

_ _ _ Anywhere after shoveling snow for seven days! – I had enough of being out in the freezing weather! – I made a promise to God! If he allowed me to get away from this place! – I will never come back again!!..

_ _ _Anyway, after coming back south to Greensboro. I applied for a student loan; and was accepted here at A.T. and T. the rest is history! I met and saw this young pretty girl! Standing up on a hill side. There, I fell head – over heel! In love with her_ _ _ (I end saying).

Smiling, Say – Say whispher: "_ _ _What an incredible story Tim! – But, I am not letting you off that easy!–(Pause) Follow me back to my car!" she ordered.

I shooked my head and said: "_ _ _Coming- miss – lady!". I whisper.

On ours way back to the car. Say – Say walked a fews feet ahead. Observing from her rear. Her body, majestically portray an artistic little figure that moved each step, in such rhythm! That the average man would turn their heads; for a second look!

Her two long braids bounced – endlessly! While playing a kissing game as they touch the upper curve line of her buttocks.

I follow, as in a trance! Just watching her walk, seem to have mystical power!

_____ Twenty minutes later, we pulled up into her drive way. Turning off her car, she snap:

"_ _ _ Tim! – We got – to talk! – I know I am young and innocent! – But, I don't know how much longer I can hold out; waiting on you!" she whisper.

I reply: "_ _ _Say Say! We've gone through this before!–You know, we can't do anything – just yet!!"

She almost screamed saying: "_ _ _ Tim – o – thy! – You got to man – up! And do something to me!".

Suddenly, a voice from inside the house call out: "_ _ _ Say – Say child! – come in this house right now!",

Say – Say jumped and whisper: "_ _ _That's my dad. I goto go _ _ _

Upon her rushing off I took a deep breatha and whisper: "_ _ _ Geeeee, that was closed!"

_____The following day, N.B.C News Broadcast: '_ _ _four Negros girls killed in Birmingham ala'. When this broadcast broked. I was at my part-time job site. A small honky tonk bar and grill.

Inside, this bar were crowded; with a bunch of red necks – white men. Minutes after this broadcasters- announced about the bombing of the girls!

I saw a hairy face white man; sitting at the bar, stood-up and shouted: "_ _ _ Yip Peee – Yippee! – Four more of them vomits! Done bite the dark _ _ _".

His arrogance remark incite another man. To come forward and yelled while holding up a bottle of beer he said: "_ _ _ Lets toast! – If the good Lord wanted to! He could have created multi – color people! – But he didn't – He created us – whites to be supreme! And them N–I–G – G – E – R – S! – to be our S – L – A – V – E –S!

The crowd went wild with laughters. I stood at the end of the bar with my mop in my hand. When another red – neck got up on top of a small table. And start mocking the broadcasters: "_ _ _That's why ours good Gov. Wallace went public and say, 'Before we give into integration! – all hell will freeze over f–i – r – s – t!!! Standing there, I could have been a fly on the wall for all he care!

_____Just then, my cell phone ring. It was Say – Say: "_ _ _Tim! I am stuck in traffic! But, I am on my way!-" she pause. "_ _ _You know my fathers found himself a town house! – and he has ask Sadie and me to move in with him! –

Say – Say continue talking: "_ _ _Tim! Lord knows I love both of my parents! – But I cain't leave my mothers right now!–In the condition she's in _ _ _".

I ask: "_ _ _Is that what you told your father?". Say – Say reply: "_ _ _No! – And I've got to fine a way to tell my mother's! When we get to the hospital! – That dad's won't be at home, when she gets there!

I reply: "_ _ _ oh boy!" Say – Say then said: "_ _ _ Tim! I am coming up near your work place! – are you out front yet?". She ask.

I answer: "_ _ _Yes! I am waiting on you _ _ _!

_____Twenty minutes later, we arrived at the hospital and exit the elevator onto the 4th floor. When we enter Mrs Henry room. We found her fully dress; sitting in her wheel chair. Mrs Henry Snap – Saying: "_ _ it's about damn – time! – you got your ass here!". – Say – Say reply: " _ _ _ momma it's only 8:55!".

Mrs Henry shouted: "_ _ _ Gal! The doctor relief me at 7:01 _ _ _". Frowning Say – Say whisper. "_ _ _ Momma! I need to tell you something!".

Mrs Henry snap –saying: "_ _ _ Gal! – I got to get home and talk to John Henry! ". – Say – Say then said: "_ _ _ Momma, momma! – Dads won't be home, when we get there!

Inquisitively, Mrs Henry ask: "_ _ _Child! What do you mean; your daddys won't be home?"

Straight –forwardly, Say – Say shouted: "_ _ _Mom, dad's have lefted you!". Mrs Henry start crying and mumble: "_ _ _He can't leave me like that! – Just because I made one littler M – I – S – T – A – K – E!".

Say – Say whisper: "_ _ _Mom, I didn't want to tell you! – But, dads have himself a town house – the u – haul truck was at the house – when I left."

Mrs. Henry began sobbing, openly: "_ _ _John Henry can't do that to me!" She pause then snap and said: "_ _ _Dirty bastard! Say – Say quickly countered and said: "_ _ _ Momma!"

_____ Twenty minutes later, we arrived back at the house and found Sadie busy, packing. She stopped just long enough to say: "_ _ _Say – Say! – Daddys say for you to give me his car keys! – He will be back in 20 minutes _ _ _

Say – Say asked: "_ _ _ Girl! Ain't you gona speak to momma?". Say – Say ask.

Sadie Reply: "_ _ _Oh, hi mom, I am leaving Mom!" Sadie snap.

Say – Say snap saying: "_ _ _Girl you're one cold hearted – bitch", Say –Say shouted.

Sadie countered: "_ _ _It's not my fault, momma was caught at that motel with her drawers down."

Furious, Say – Say shouted: "_ _ _I should have whipped your ass; when I caught you with my man!".

Say –Say shouted, now moving aggressively toward Sadie. I jump between them and shouted "_ _ _Say – Say, beating her ass won't settler anything!"

Mrs Henry maneuver her wheel chair around and yelled: "_ _ _ Say – Say! Give this heifer those keys; so she can get her blk – ass out-of-here!" Mr. Henry whisper.

_____ After Sadie had walk away Mrs. Henry whisper: "_ _ _ I hate to admit, Sadie was telling the truth! I was caught with my drawers down! But, I wouldn't had to do it; if John Henry was taking care of his home work!

Embarrased, Say – say whispered. "_ _ _Momma! You don't has to explain anything to us". Say – say whisper

Mrs. Henry whisper back in a low breathe: "_ _ _child! I've got to get this off my chest! (pause) Lord, how am I gona make it without John Henry??" she cried.

Say –Say then voiced: "_ _ _Momma, the lord will make – a – way, some how!" Say – Say whisper.

_____Minutes later, Sadie call from out front: "_ _ _Momma, daddy is back_ _ _". Sadie yelled.

Say –Say whisper, saying: "_ _ _ I thought Sadie was gone!". Mrs Henry whisper: _ _ _me too! (before yelling) Sadie! Ask your father to come in a minutes"

Mr. Henry enter, when Mrs. Henry asked: "_ _ _John Henry we need to talk!" Mr. Henry didn't made eyes contact reply. "_ _ _ woman! There ain't nothing you and I need to talk about_ _ _"

While dis-regarding what mister Henry had just said Mrs. Henry shouted: "_ _ _John Henry! – why would you just leave me like that??". Mrs. Henry ask.

Mr. Henry shouted – back: "_ _ _The same damn's way you left your home; and went and f_ _k that man!". Mrs. Henry pled: "_ _ _That ain't fair John Henry! – That man didn't mean a – thing, to me!!

Mister Henry whisper again: "_ _ _woman! – all of your talking now! – is dirt water under the bridge!". Turning he yelled "_ _ _ Sarah- child! – if you want to, you can come too!".

While Mr. Henry walked out the door. Mrs Henry shouted: "_ _ _John Henry! – you can't leave me like this! – (pause) I – am – sorry!!" she whisper_ _ _

_____ Two days later, Say – Say and I had a third luncheon engagement at the Moon – Glo. Today, she seem different. Her bi –polar disorder wasn't dominating her behavers she appeared to be functioning at a Norm!

Today, at a table inside this restaurant. Say – Say – start the conversation about an event-remark made by a negro leaders: "_ _ _ Tim! Did you hear that racial remark; made by that black activate??". I answer "_ _ _No, I didn't!".

Say – say then said: "_ _ _well, this colored – brother said that president kennedys- assassination was no more than a case of the chickens coming home to roost! And when chickens come home to roost!- They always made him glad! _ _ _

I look at Say – Say in disbelief and reply: "_ _ _that wasn't a nice thing to say about Mr. Kennedy's and I know, he wasn't speaking on behalf of most black folks!". I whisper "_ _ _definitely, not for me!". Say – Say reply. Change subject and ask: "_ _ _Tim! – when will you makes love to me?".

I reply: "_ _ _Say – Say! we've gone through this before_ _ _!

_____About that time, this waitress came back to ours table. And shouted:"_ _ _Little girl, you're just fresh out of diapers!

– Asking this man to make love to you! – You ought to be ar – shame! _ _ _

Say –Say stood – up and shouted: "_ _ _- Look bitch! There's ain't no shame, in my wanting to make love_ _ _!!

This waitress then look at Tim and Reply: "_ _ _Handsome, when time come for you to make love! – I'll be more then glad to turn you on!"

Her words were like putting salt in the wound, to Say – Say. Reaching, Say – Say delivered an open hand blow. To this waitress face; causing her serving tray to fall onto the floor. "_ _ _ oh shit! – This bitch just slap me!". This waitress screamed.

Meanwhile, a costumer at another table yelled: "_ _ _you better call the poor – poor!". I call out to Say – Say: "_ _ _let's get the hell out of here! – Now pulling onto Say – Say arm.

_____We ran severals blocks before stopping. When we did, I shouted: "_ _ _Say – Say I can't believe you slap that woman!" Say – Say snapped and say: "_ _ _Believe it! I never like to bitch anyway! – (pause) and she had the nerves to say she will turn you on _ _ _!".

I tried saying; "_ _ _But honey!" Say – say snapped. "_ _ _Don't you but honey me! Right now I am a littler frustrated and horny. I reach over, passionately – kissing Say – Say.

She push me away and whisper: "_ _ _Tim! – You just don't know how much pressure. Have build-up inside of me! (pause) And, I don't know how to handle it! _ _ _". She then stood and whisper: "_ _ _ Timothy! – would you take me home?". I start kissing her again. This time, she shouted. "_ _ _ -Timothy! – Got – damned, stop teasing me; It's too damned hot for that".

Smiling I whisper: "_ _ _you're sweating on your nose! – people who sweat on their nose; are said to be mean!!". She then mimic calling out my name.

I whisper: "_ _ _Geeee, you're one beautiful, cho-co-late – brown skin W – O – M – A – N!".

_____Leaving the Park; Which was located just south of CAMPUS. And about ten blocks from Say – Say house. We began walking through some of this city worst ghetto. This Area was so poverty – stricken!

That the evidence of drugs and prostitutions were advertised on every street corner. After walking some five blocks Say – Say, violent out-burst, seem to have settle. That surge of Anger; had sub-side back to that sweet littler girl. I knew! Twenty minutes later, we made it to her front door. She ask: "_ _ _ TIM! – Will you come in for a spell?" – I shook my head and lied- saying:" _ _ _ I can't, I need to get back and study for an Exam!" She casually dismiss my rejection saying: " _ _ _ O.K then, I guess I'll talk to you later _ _ _ " _____ Colored- people, The story continue. By the time most of the political turmoil had settle from the Assasination of President Kennedy's. Vice President Johnson had officially serve out the remaining terms for President Kennedy's.

After Mister Johnson was elective on his owns (under his administration). A civil rights, three acts were passed by congress that barred most racial discrimination in all places of public accommodation.

Theses acts, (1964 – 65 and 66) were a slap-in the faces to whites! Especially here in Greensboro. Today, hundreds of poor whites; took to the streets. In retaliation against the passing of these new laws!

A group known as the Ku – Klux – Klans! Were spear – head – ing a demonstration. That was mix with a group of Greens – boro most aggressive – seg – regationer's!

Today, as they violently rampage wildly through the streets! Singing loudly, their slogans – insults: " _ _ _ Two – four – six – eight! – we don't want to inte- gated! – Two – four – six – eight!! – we don't want to in – te – gated – Two _ _ _ ".

As they marchs, encounterings every black person along the way. They brutally beat, and in some instancy, killed that isolated black person most threat – ening!

They continue sing – ing: " _ _ _ Two – four – six – eight _ _ _ !" As they storm through this south side Littler multicultural neighborhood. They confronted and attack! Killing the field secretary of the: N. A. A.C.P. (Mister John Henry). On his way to his car one of the rioters yelled: " _ _ _ Kill that uncle – Tom looking S. O. B! _ _ _ "

When the news broked of Mr. Henry killing. I was in my dorm's room. Studying for an up-coming exam. Sadie call me and urgently, ask could I meet her at the Emergency hospital. Something about Say – Say!

Rushing, 20 minutes later. I stormed into the E.M.S. where Sadie met me. And shouted:" _ _ _ Mr. Timothy! – I am glad you could come! – Them red-necks done slaughter my dads! – They beat and killed him; like, he was a dog! – They killed him – they killed him _ _ _ she sobbed.

I interrupt Sadie and whisper: " _ _ _ Sadie! – I am sorry to hear about your fathers! But what about Say – Say?", I ask.

Sadie then whisper: " _ _ _ oh, she had a seizure! – And pass out shortly after I got – up here! – That was when I call you! "

Again, I asked: " _ _ _ Sadie! You still haven't told me tet! – Where is Say – Say??? – Sadie then said: " _ _ _ OH, I think they moved her up to room 2-0-4! For a temporary – observation??

I then said; " _ _ _ Sadie, don't you think we should go up and check on her? _ _ _ "

Sadie then reply: " _ _ _ That may be a bad ideal!"

_____Up in room 2-0-4 when Sadie and I first reach Say – Say. She appeared delusional. She didn't even recognize me. While standing at her bed side.

I whisper:"_ _ _ Say – Say honey! How are you feeling? ", I ask. Puzzled, she ask:"_ _ _ Who are you?"

I then shouted:"_ _ _ Sarah! It's me, Tim – o – thy! " she said: " _ _ _ Is that you daddys?? "she ask.

Nervously, I shouted again: "_ _ _ Sarah! – Look at me honey; Don't you know me? ", I ask.

Sadie then Snap – and Say: " _ _ _ This bitch done flip! – Crazy as hell!!"

_____ Just then, The doctor walk back into the room and whisper: " _ _ _This Gal! Just experience a seizure! She maybe a littler bit! – out of it right now!"

Unfamiliars to this medical term. I ask: "_ _ _ Doc! – would you run that by me again? " – This doctor's then reply: " _ _ _ That's an abnormal – electrical – discharge in the brain that sometime could cause a patent to blank out!

Inquistively, I ask:"_ _ _ Doctor! – Is it cure- able?? "

This doctor citied:"_ _ _ young man, with plenty of love and rest! – I believe she will be just fine! – But, for now I suggest you'll go and take her home! – There's nothing more, this hospital can do for her, right now _ _ _ (Doctor exit)

As the doctor walk away, Sadie whisper: "_ _ _ come on Tim! Let's take this crazy – ass girl home _ _ _

I counted:"_ _ _ Sadie! Don't say that, your sister isn't crazy!" I whisper

Sadie reply: "_ _ _ If you say so Tim! But, if she's quacking like a duck! And acting like a stupid duck! – Then, she must be C – RA – ZY!"

_____ The brutal killing of N.A.A.C.P field representatives had Attract attention. All the way, Up to the white house, Greensboro had capture the spot light; As being, one of the most intense cities!

Today, because of such large audiences. Mr. Henry funeral was held at the local high school gymnasium. Where, his wife, Mrs Henry, Conduct the Eulogy _ _ _

Sitting there, at the Pulpit. In her wheel chair. Her frail body, resemble a picture of a broken – woman! Her eyes depict, that she has ice waters. Running all through her veins!

As she clear her throat, She commence:"_ _ _ The Lord giveth and the Lord taketh away! – Bless be the name of the Lord! – (PAUSE) John Henry spend his Entire adult life! – Fighting these whites – SUPREMACISTS! – He Labor in the picket lines! Demonstratings his dis – approval of _____ S-E-G-R-E-G-A-T-I-O-N! (She pause again)

_ _ _ You see, my John Henry wasn't a recreational demonstrators! – John eat, sleep seeking after civil rights!

_ _ _ My John Henry sacrifice his life rebelling against Jim Crows! Even, during times when he was put in Jail! His Family went Liking! – still John stay the course! – seeking after civil rights _ _ _

Mrs Henry pause a third time while maneuering her wheel chair closer to the microphone. Now wiping tears from her eyes. She citied:"_ _ _ severals evening ago! – A group of cowardly – white – men! – went undercover; and took sheets, putting them over theirs heads! – They went out into the streets! Looking to slaughter every black person – They came across!

_ _ _ (She pause again). " Theses cowards ran across my John Henry! – on his way to his car! (sobbing openly). They butchered him in the worst – kind of way! – They didn't just kill him! – They over – killed him!! – Leaving his body on the side of the street – like a dog!

All because he was B-L-A-C-K _ _ _ Mrs Henry spoked that day for 30 minutes. Before concluding:" _ _ I didn't come here today! – To just eulogize and bury my husband! I came to resurrect that awaking – awareness! – My John Henry had – to seek after civil rights!

And hopefully,–I might inbred that awareness of John Henry! – Into each of your hearts! – To go out and tell this sick – white – world's – that until black folks be given theirs civil – rights!

There won't be any peace or transquility in these land _ _ _". (She End).

_____ After the funeral, down town Greensboro came under attack. There were mass Rioting, dozens of municipal office buildings were set on firer! Hundreds of negros demonstrator's stormed police – precinct.

Some were throwing red paint ball pellets! – While other, demanded that an arrest be made! In the killing of N.A.A.C.P. – Secretary. Theses demonstrations continue there, in Greensboro for weeks _ _ _

_____ Over the next several months. Say – say illness took a term for the worst! She began experience back – to – back seizures. Her psychotic disorder, had now triggered multiple – personalities.

_ _ _ When it rain, it pours! Here, we have a perfectly sound minded young lady one day and the next day. Her mind takes on multiple – Characters!

I was so – concern about Say – Say condition. I cancel three of my classes. So I could be there; To help take care of her. Anyway, on this particular day. Shortly after Say – Say had a recurrent seizures. (blank – out)

Sadie shouted: " _ _ _ Oh my God Tim! This gal done flipped out again!" Sadie screamed – I counter saying: " _ _ _ Sadie! – Put her head up on the Pillar!"

While putting Say – Say head up on the pillar. Sadie reached over, touching my hand. And start whispering a proposition: " _ _ _ Tim! I've been waiting for this chance! – A long time! – ". Bending over Say – Say dead body! – Sadie bury her tongue within my mouths.

Overwhelm, I snatch my head away! – Suddenly, Say – Say came up swin- ing! – Sucker punchs – Sadie in the fore – head. The impact knocked Sadie backward. Her head collided with the sharpe edge of the dresser.

I screamed: " _ _ _ Jesus – christ Say – Say! – I think you killed her; She is not moving! ".

Say – Say casually whisper:" _ _ _ I told that winch, to stay away from you!" she pause, then ask. " _ _ _ Who are you??".

I snap – saying: " _ _ _ Not again Say -Say! – Girl you need help! – " My loud shouting must have triggered another personality – character's in her. She ask: " _ _ _ Man! – Why are you shouting? ".

I again snap – and ask:" _ _ _ What about your sister Sadie? ". I ask Say- Say casually whisper:" _ _ _ What about Sadie! I supposed we need to call the police _ _ _ Say – Say voice change again!

" _ _ _ Tim! – Which Police killed my sister!". She ask – I yelled:" _ _ _ Say – Say! You killed your sister!!" My screaming triggered still another characters! –" _ _ _ Is the bitch dead?" This voice ask.

I end, saying:" _ _ _ Girl, you got it bad _ _ _!

_____ Fortunately, for Say – Say sake. Sadie death was ruled a suicide. After Mrs. Henry had conspired; Giving the police evidence of a suicide note. That was written by Sadie. When she was incarcerated. (The note) : ' _ _ _ Stop this world, I want to get off! – I can't take this life any longer! "Sign – Sadie Joyner!

Mrs. Henry lied, when she told investigaters. That her daughter's had been under a lot of stress! Most of her life! – And this note, was the second note her child had written _ _ _

_____ Sadie death made the second funeral. This Joyners – family had inducer in the past six months. Yet, unlike Mr. Henry funeral and at Mrs. Henry request. She wanted a private funeral for Sadie.

There would be no burying ceremony. No Funeral directors. In fact, After the coroners – in Quest: Mrs Henry hired a Pizza – delivery man; To transport the body. To the burial site.

_____ At the grave site only a handful of family members were present. Mrs Henry spoked the following words: " _ _ _ Lord, here lies the body of a child! – maybe it would have been best! That she was never born! (she pause) _ _ _ I birth this gal into this world! After I had been rape! – on my wedding day!

-You see, she and my baby daughters Sarah! Are twins! – Tho they have differerence fathers!"

_____ Sobbing now Say – Say standing nearby whisper. " MOMMA! Must you tell all this now? " Mrs Henry held up both hand and Continue

" _ _ _ Yes child! – I need to get this off my chest. Before I put this heifers in the ground! (Pause). Like I just said! – I was secretly rape on the same day – just hours before I consummate myself! To my husband, John Henry! –

She pause again " _ _ _ _ This bastard who rape me! – Be her fathers, and my husband John Henry is your fathers, honey!". She pointed " _ _ _ This heifers came straight out of my womb, feets first! – kicking and bitting her sister!! _ _ _

Say – Say voiced out loud: " _ _ _ so that explain why Sadie hated me so!??

Mrs Henry continue: " _ _ _ kicking and bitting onto her sister! – I knew right then. She was a devil – child from hell! (She pause one last time).

_ _ _ Go on, my one time daughters! – Go on, from ashes to ashes! – From – dust to dust!! _ _ _

Meanwhile, this pizza delivery man start lowering the body bag into the ground.

Say – Say whisper: " _ _ _ so long heifers!" Mrs Henry mumble, "_ _ _ Say – Say! – Have some respect for your sisters; Even through she wasn't worst a shit _ _ _

_____ Sadie was laid to rest in this black cemetery. Where many of the graves – site. Had head – stone, of tree – block. That were over – lay with concrete.

Meanwhile, over on the north side of the city. A group of black demonstrators were in a fourth week of protesting the killing of N.A.A.C.P fallen – hero.

Today, what started out as a peaceful protest. Had escalate after four hours. Into a full blown riots! – It was believe that many of the local demonstrators; Had call, A- quit, for today. L eaving behind those out of towners! Die- hard protestor's – trouble – maker's! Whom had come to Greensboro! Only, to steer – up trouble.

As this group moved along this predominate white neighborhood. Throwing rocks, bottles destroying some of this exclusive homes. They sang: '_ _ _ Black – Lifes – Matter – Black – Lifes – Matter – Blk. – Lifes – Matter_ _ _ ' Approaching Crawford road extension. This crowd were confront by a small group of heavily armored klansmens.

Up, ahead these klansmen had fortify. A barricade – human wall of themselves! – All combat

Ready! Suddenly. A voice shouted from behind that barricade wall: " _ _ _ Stop , Stop! All you niggers are walking on shakey ground! – Turn around, and takes you blacks assess home!!"

One of the blk. demonstrator's yelled and ask: "_ _ _ which one of you, son – of – a – bitches! – Shot and killed ours un- armored brother?"

It was then when one klansman; stepped out front of their barrificade wall and shouted: ' _ _ _ All of us share in killing that black bastard!" he brag. Meanwhile, another blk demonstrators ask; " _ _ _ why – white boy? ? "

Smiling now, this klansman shouted: " _ _ _ Because he was black! – And we needed something to do !!" His answer was like, pouring Salt in on an open wounds. Just then, The leaders from the black demonstrators yelled: " _ _ _ Move aside white boy! We're com – ing through! – S–T–A–M–P–E–D–E _ _ _ "

_____ What happen next, could best be describe: As the Massacre at littler – big – horn! – The destruction lifes! Were so drastic. One local news paper ran a head-line; _ _ _ shocked – and – horrify _ _ _ '

During the confrontation, 125 demonstrators were injury. Five were killed. Still, two dozens or more blk demontrator's. Forced theirs way through the barricade wall. Rushing, six blocks up onto the steps of police headquarter. Where they were confronted again, this time by a barricade wall of policemen. Who arrested them; For in- citing a riot!

_____ Looking back, There have always been an up hill struggle among black people. It all got started, the minute ours African ancestry got off those slaves ship.

_ _ _ For the following 150 years. Black folks had labor through blood, sweat and tears! Build – this country. Generation after generations of blk. People have fought against slavery! To a nation of people that found this country on the creed, That all men are created equally!

_ _ _ A Lie, they declare!! While walking through the foot prints of slavery! This white – race have always advocate theirs views on slavery. That owning slaves, were theirs god – given right!

This controversy triggered a civil war. Where white men, North and South of the mason – dixie. Dispute theirs cause! Theses debates went on for years. In fact, Mr. Lincoln came to fame; debating the slave issued. Although many historians had written that Mr. Lincoln emancipated slaves! His only objective, was about keeping the country together!

And Mr. Lincoln used, freeing slaves. As a Level to win the war!

_____ After the North won the war. Many confederate white men came home and found theirs farms land in ruins. All their slaves gone! And, having to content with the new Law of Emancipation.

Having to deal with this re-construction; and facing the black man. As his equal, was more then theses whites – boys could endure!

Soon, theses whites boys empowered them-selves saying: " _ _ _ There is a new sheriff in town! – And his name is Jim – Crows! _ _

They conspired a set of Laws! Which practice a policy of segregation; To demoralize blacks! Their's tactic employed, going out into the streets disguising themselves with sheets. Intimidating, beating, sometimes killing blacks. Into a living nightmare!

With the absent of federal troops. Many blacks, at the time had came to the relization that this is a white man worlds; And blacks, just got to tried and live in it!

Unfortunately, This next generation of blk wasn't ready to turn the other cheek! In defiance, they proclaim " Black lifes – matter! Blk – lifes matter!!

_____ This new generation of blacks were willing to stand in the mid of oppression and fight at all cost such cases as: _ _ _ The case involving those three black panthers – who was accused of that mass killings! At the grayhound bus station. They were tried and sentence to electro – cution!

_ _ _The case of the arrest of James Crawford attorneys were able to pull the broard – cast foots – tages which clearly show Mr.

Crawford – standing in the front row – Through- out the entire inter – view! His case was thrown – out _ _ _

_ _ _ The case of the widows – whom husband was slayed! Today, she filed a three millions dollars law – suit! Against the K.K.K organization! It was the talk of the town one local news reporter's wrote: _ _ _ All there turbulence – times. Can best be describe as black – eye pea!! Which simply means, a bruising – episode – in human relationship _ _ _

_____ Today, over in Civil – court Mrs Henry attorneys were presenting their case against three klans members. Everyone knew, there wasn't a chance – in hell! These white – men, would be convicted! But then too, everyone knew the world were monitoring the out – come! His opening statement: " _ _ _ Might I remind the court! That my client, John Henry have that same personal – rights of protection! Guaranteed by the 13th and 14th amendment! Of the constitution! (he pause) But, mister Henry is no longer with us today! Thank to this crew – of – prejudice – scums!

This Judge intervene: " _ _ _ would you get to the point boy! " , This Judge shouted.

This Attorney whisper: " _ _ _ Your honor Sir! I hate to play the race – card! But the only reason my clients was killed! Is because, he was black! _ _ _ "

This Judge intervene again: " _ _ _ Boyy! I would not allow you to come in my court room! Playing the race – card and attacking these outstanding men!

This Judge continue: " _ _ _ and unless you can present some reasonable cause! – Why this case should continue! – I am gona rule, A mis – trial! "

The Attorney for Mrs Henry shouted: " _ _ _ Your honor – sir! – Before you declare a mis-trial! – I've several credible witness, ready to take the stand _ _ _ "

_____ Before this trial End. This attorney presentive the court with all of the evidence it need, to win. After hours of litigation. Mrs Henry was awarded 3,000,000 dollars in damages against the K.K.K organization.

This lawsuit left the klansmen Penniless. Their cash – assets bank – ruptured! In executing this settlement. The Klans – organization paid out in cash, Two millions – seven – hundreds – thousands – dollars piece of property. That have a two story building on site. This building once, had been the klans headquarter!

_____ After receiving this settlement. Mrs Henry quickly transfer the deed of the building over to the N.A.A.C.P. as an award. The N.A.A.C.P used the building for their headquarters. Smiling, Mrs Henry mumble: " _ _ _ Most embarrassing for these whites boys! – After all, It's the lease I could do! – To get revenge, for them killing my John Henry! " she mumble out loud.

Mrs. Henry didn't stop there. She negotiate de a deal. Where she hired a Lawyer's firm; Paying them $100, 000 dollars. To represent each of the demonstrator's. In theirs court cases. A move she thought would help the blk movement _ _ _

_____ Frustrated, City mayors was upset over the number of demonstrations. And, all the mass destruction of public property.

Today, Greensboro City mayors had petition the governor's. In sending 500 civil service troops to help local law enforcement. To go out in this south side neighborhood. And root out, those criminals; And bring them to Justice _ _ _

_____ It was my last day before my graduation. Say – Say and I walk along side the bared wire barricade. That stretch full length around this south side neighborhood. This placed, kind – of remind me of a war – zone Say- Say whisper: " _ _ _ it's a damned shame, these – niggers had to burn down theirs own's neighborhood! "

I reply: " _ _ _ That's nothing compare to that 150 blocks area! – This other blk group burns down in South – western L .A !" , I citied.

Say – Say whisper: " _ _ _ Humm, cutting off their noses to spike their faces; is not the answer! " She whisper.

I citied: " _ _ _ Hummm, tried telling that to the 34 persons – who was killed! (Pause) The L .A time news paper reported that the loss due to looting, firer and other willfull destructions were estimated in excess of 40 millions dollars!" Say – Say then said. " _ _ _ There have got to be another way! – Blk people can express ourselves! – To achieve our civil right! "

I whisper: " _ _ _ I don't know Say – Say! But you must admit these demonstrations! Have gotten the white man attention!"

Say – Say said: " _ _ _ How? – By destroying and killing your owns; Tim! – That's deffenselessly, not the way! "

I snap – saying: " _ _ _ Say – Say! You should be the last person; To talk about killing your owns kind! "

Frowning, Say – Say reply: " _ _ _ O.K Tim! – Maybe I asked for that! – But Sadie had it coming! "

_____ We came up to that opening in the barricade fence. Just outside, A small group of students; were protesting their hostility against the governor's. For sending troops into the black community. As we cross their picket – line. Say- Say, hurriedly grib my hand and whisper:

" _ _ _ Tim! – come tomorrow this time! – You will have your diploma – ticket ! – And ready to get away from all this mess _ _ _ "

I end our conversation, saying: " _ _ _ Say – Say! – I am gona miss this place _ _ _ "

_____ It took a long time coming. After four tiresome years. Today, at my commencement – graduation. A.T. and T had hired the President. From South Carolina state college. To be ours key note speakers.

President Corbins spoked on the topic. "White – superiorty! " _ _ _ Greet – ing and Salutations! – To all my black brothers and sisters!

Soon, Each of you will leave this Auditorium today! And enter a world – where the white man! Had declare themselves superior!

_ _ _ And without doubt! – Most of you will go out in search of a Job! – That is within your field! – Please – be aware! – After you apply and in some instances over – qualify! – For that Job! – Your chances of getting that Job–Compare to your white counter – part! – Will be slim to none!!

_ _ _ I stop by here today! – To tell you'll! – If you'll are lucky enough to get that Job! – I am talking about that same Job. – That your white counter – Part might apply for! – Your salaries will be relatively lower then your white counter part! – All! Because of the color of your skin! _____

Please – don't be dis-courages! – Press on toward the mark!

President Corbin's spoked for 30 minutes before concluding:

_ _ _ I challenge each of you! – To boldly stand – firms – against racial oppression! – With your one weapon! – Which is your education! – Please, please be not dismays! – Press on toward the mark_ _ _

_____ After hearing President corbin's speaks. I had chills bumps running down my neck I was honor, to have Say – Say and her mother's to attend. Upon leaving, MRS Henry surprise me; And books reservation for Dinner. At one of those big name steak houses.

At the Restaurant table. I said: " _ _ _ Mrs Henry, I am most appreciative! – That you thought enough of me, to do this _ _ _ " – Mrs Henry Respond. " _ _ _ Tim, it's the least I could do! – Beside, You're like Family _ _ _ ".

Jokenly, Say – Say added: " _ _ _ Mom! – He is almost like, he has been shacking with our family! – He's at the house most of the time " she Joked _ _ _

_____ After this waitdress brought our meals. Say- Say cellphone sounded

She had it on speaker. It was someone calling from E.R! To informed the family. That 76 yrs. Old mother of MRS Henry was just qunned down. At the radio station _ _ _ MRS Henry was a civil rights activate!

When Mrs Henry over-heard the conversation. She snatch the cell phone and shouted: "_ _ _Doctor! – will she be O.K?" The voice on the other end of the phone reply: "_ _ _Right now, she have a 50/50 chance of surviving through the night! (pause)_ _ _I am sorry ma!'" the voice echo.

Sobbing while hanging up the phone. Mrs Henry mumble: "_ _ Lord, what am I gona do now! I can't take care of momma, from this wheel chair" she sobbed.

Say – say countered: "_ _ _well momma, there ain't no one else, but uncle Toney!" Say – Say whisper.

Mrs Henry Mumble: "_ _ _child, your uncle Tony's! Is all the way up in Colorado!".

Say – Say snap – saying: "_ _ _well momma, uncle Tony may have to quit the police – Job! – and bring his ass home, to help you_ _ _".

That was when I said: "_ _ _ Say – Say, you didn't tell me you have an uncle! Who's a policeman_ _ _!"

Frowning, Say – Say answer: "_ _ _ yes, uncle Tony is the last living brother. My momma have left! (pause)_ _ _anyway, back some years ago! – Uncle Toney got hooked up with this white girl! – Somehow, her family found out about theirs affair! – when, this white girl fathers threaten to kill uncle Toney! _ _ _That was when uncle Tony's and this white chick! Ran away up north and got marry – since that time, uncle Tony been in Colorada, working as a policeman_ _'

I then whisper: "_ _ _Say – Say!

I am impress_ _ _!

_____News of the shooting of G – Momma – Joyners. Had been investigated by the F.B.I Theirs intelligent report, reveals that this small terrorisms group; that attack the radio station. Were ex – klans members. Two, which had previously been indicted for all those black men killed.

Farther investigation reveal that at lease six members of the K.K.K. had infiltrate Greensboro Police department. And were acting under orders of chief portee. On a execution mission! The big pay back against the Joyner's family!

_____ Today, after five weeks and two days. In the hospital Mrs Joyners was coming home her flamboyant – manner, as a talk – show host had called out some of Greensboro most extreme – segregationers.

During Mrs Joyners 40 years talk – show. She has attack Jim Crow! As a segregationer's – bully. Un – fortunately, these Jim Crow alien had counter – attack her. Leaving her paralyze, now she have to go home and live with her disable daughters! Who was also wheel chair bounded.

Meanwhile, down in the hospital lobby. G – momma – Joyner's was confronted by a small crew of news reporters. One reporter ask: "_

_ _Mrs Joyners! – what are the chances of returning one day; back to host your talk show?".

About that time Mrs Henry's had her chauffer's drivers. To hurriedly ushered her head long into the crews of reporters and snap – saying: "_ _ _Gentlemen, my mother's not gona answer anymore questions!", Mrs Henry snap. Another reporters push forward and say. "_ _ _But, Mrs Henry! The public have the right to know these things!"

As the Limousine spede away. Several reporter's follow 20 minutes later, they pulled up into the drive way. Where they were met again by another group of reporter's.

When G –Momma – Joyners got out of the Limousine one reporters ask: "_ _ _Mrs Joyner, Do you know who shot you?" Before answering, another reporter ask "_ _ _Mrs Joyner, now that you've been wounded! – Have you change your views on civil rights? _ _ _".

Mrs Joyners almost came up out of her wheel chair. Shouted: "_ _ _Just because I am in this wheel chair! – It don't change a thing! – (pause) and you can tell those yellow – belly! That shot me! – They haven't heard the last from me yet!!_ _ _

_____ Severals days later. Say – Say had a one – on – one littler talk with her mother. "_ _ _Momma now that you have this money! – are you gona sit there on your blk. ass; and do nothing! _ _ _

Mrs Henry answered: "_ _ _That's for me to know; and your blk. ass to find out". Mrs Henry snap.

Say – Say countered: "_ _ _ Momma, I was just asking cause Tim and I been talking about shacking – up!".

Mrs Henry shouted: "_ _ _child! Why give that man the cow before the calf??", she ask.

Say – Say snap – saying: "_ _ _Because momma! There's not gona be no calf's! – Besides, we're tired of secretly sleeping around!_ _ _" Say – Say shouted.

Mrs Henry then said: "_ _ _ Go ahead child! – You're gona do what you want to do anywhere!".

Say – say then whisper: "_ _ _Momma! – My real concern is leaving you alone with G – momma!" _ _

Mrs Henry ended saying: "_ _ _ Go ahead child! Beside, it won't be long before your uncle Tony get here!"_ _ _

_____ During the following few weeks. While living together both wheel chairs bound! These two colored women talks extensively about theirs retaliated plans against segregation. Mrs Joyner's ask: "_ _ _ Shirley, I know it's none of my business! But, what's your plans on getting back at those honkies! Who killed John Henry??" Mrs Joyners ask.

Mrs Henry reply: "_ _ _No Momma! Its ain't none of your business! – But, if you must know; I've already humiliated the klansmen! (pause) when I their head quarters building – and gaved it to the N.A A.C.P. _ _ _

Mrs Joyner's then said: Shirley – child! – That's not enough! I think you can do morer!". Mrs Joyner's whispered. Mrs Henry add – saying" _ _ _I've also paid out $100,000 for legal fees; for all those demonstrator's and, (she pause agan) _ _ _ I am running for that vacant seat on city – council!".

_____ The Joyners family had been on the front line – fight for civil rights! For as far back as I could remember. Their on – g-0 – ing struggle wasn't just against segregation.

At the time, there was a social barriers; within the negro race. Apparently, there were those oppity high yellow group. Whom had excel above their fellow – brothers. Now, had segregate themselves in their own littler churches, schools and businesses.

_____ In Colorado, when precinct captain gaved officer Joyners that type written telegraph. He knew right away, what he had to do. _ _ _To give – up his job; and move back south.

Ultimately, his biggest concern was having to move back south with a white wife and a 19 yrs old son. Whom had return back from the war, mentally wounded!

_ _ _of course, all these concerns had taken a back – row. Now, that his mothers needed his help!

(Rememinicing)

Shortly after littler Tony Joyners came back from the war with so many un-explained circumstances.

Officers Joyners took it upon him self; and made an inquiry in his son service record.

Upon inquiry, officers Joyners found that the U.S Army kepted a segregated set of records. For blacks and whites soldiers. Below is a trans script copy of Lance Corporal Record: '_ _ _on this __day 19 teens hundred and __ Lance Corporal Tony Joyners Jr. was shot in the head – while on the battler field –

During surgery ours doctors discovered Lance Corporal Tony Joyners Jr. was infective with the asia's – orange virus! And most possibly Aid!

_ _ _Farther, Lance Corporal Tony Joyners Jr. – Is hearby discharge with full honor from the U.S Army_ _ _

_____Corporal Joyner's return home to his parents, an asylums – man! Each day now, Joyners could be seen sitting on his parents front porch. In his rocking chair. Puffing away on his marijuana pipe_ _ _

Meanwhile, a white supremacist – group were rallyings in the streets against this black life's – matter group. Their war – cry were: '_ _ _white – lifes – matter – too'.

As they marchs, while exciting racial – insults they were encounter by a squadron of policemen.

Attempting to make an arrest; of this arrogant – out – spoken supremacist – leaders. Official Joyners led his unit; in the raid. Called – out: "_ _ _T.H. finth! You're under arrest! – ", Joyners yelled.

Now pulling away, finth voiced "_ _ _What for, colored–boy?", Finth snap and ask_ _ _

Official Joyners snap – back and said: "_ _ _For inciting a riot, among other_ _ _'

_____ The last thing, this city need right now. Is another disturbance between blacks and whites! Especially after all of the young blk. men killings!

Today was Joyners last day on the job. TT had been six weeks. Since he filed papers, to retired.

After renting a small u – haul – trailer. Joyners and his family was finally ready to make that cross country trip to Greensboro.

Twelve hours later the Joyner's cross the Greensboro city – limited – line. Mr Joyner's whisper: "_ _ _Honey! This city haven't change very much; since we left!",

Mrs Joyners answer, while sitting in the rear seat: "_ _ _I know Jim! That's why I choose to ride back here! And let Juniors ride up front _ _ _".

Mr. Joyners then said: "_ _ _ Good choice honey! – cause we don't want no trouble with the P – O- L – I – I – C – E !!", he laughs.

That was when Tony Jr. shouted: "_ _ _ Mother – _____ the P – O – L – I – C – E!!"

Mrs Joyners snap – saying: "_ _ _ Tony – honey – we're in Jim crows country now! These whites folks down here; don't take too kindly to mix marriages!!", she whisper.

Mr Joyners add: "_ _ _ Tony son! Listen to your mothers! These policemen down here operate much difference then back in Colorado!".

Tony looked across at his father's and snap: "_ _ _Dad! What are you trying to say? – Now, that we're in the south! – I got to spend the rest of my life; walking on eggs shell??". Tony ask.

Mr Joyners said: "_ _ _No son, what I am trying to say! – Is, if you don't put some handle on your mouth! – You won't be around down here for long!" Mr Joyners shouted.

Frowning, Tony snap – saying: "_ _ _I still say, mother_____ the police!!" _ _

Mr Joyner's end – saying: "_ _ _ o.k son! – we'll leave this talk right here for now_ _ _".

_____ Shortly after officer Joyner's came back. He tooked half of his 401 – K retirement fund and purchase a three bedroom town house. In a mix neighborhood.

And just when every thing seem to be working out. Mrs Joyner's father, who lived just three houses down the street. Bo gart his way into her house; confronting her, he shouted: " _ _ _Hey child! It have been a long – ass time! – I heard you got your self a black son!".

Mrs Joyner snap – saying: "_ _ _yess dad! He's grown now! (pause) He's sitting right over there; on the other side of the porch!", she pointed.

Her father snap saying: "_ _ _Oh no child! I don't want to meet no nigger!! He snap _ _ _

Frowning, Mrs Joyner's snap – saying: "_ _ _Dad, you haven't change a bit! – I think you should leave_ _ _" she whisper.

_____ Today, the N. A. A. C P. had team – up with Greensboro black – local radio station. To honor Mrs Joyner, on her civil rights achievement. In today event, she will be given the, 'woman- of – the year award'.

This day – long gathering was schedule with a kick – off speech deliver by Mrs Joyner. Follow by a demonstration – sit – ins! At severals down town lunch counters.

(24 hours earlier)_ Mrs Henry was suppose to coordinate and make the preparation; to inform her mother that she was being honor at tomorrow event: "_ _ _Hello Jim, this is Shirley! – How about doing me a favor! – Tell momma she's being honor! – and she got to delivers a speech on tomorrow_ _ _"

Jim intervene saying: "_ _ _ Shirley, momma is sitting right here; why don't you tell her yourself!", Jim snap – saying.

Mrs Joyner over heard the conversation. Snatch the cell phone and shouted: "_ _ _Shirley! Just because I am paralyze in this chair! – Don't mean I can't hear or speak for myself!!", Mrs Joyners voiced.

Shirley reply: "_ _ _Oh Momma! I wasn't trying to dis –respect you in any way!".

Furious now, Mrs Joyners snap: "_ _ _ Shirley – child! – next time you call over here with information about me! – please, talk to me first!!", she snap.

_____24 hours later. In this outdoor city park. Mrs Joyner's maneuver her wheel chair up behind this cement design podium. While flamboyant – waving to the crowd. She began speaking: "_ _ _Greeting – greeting! – Yess them bucklers thought they had taken – me out! – when they, so cowardly! – shot me in the back! (she smiled) Hell! My grandma can shoot better than that! (pause)_ _ _Yes they thought they had put me six feet under! – But look you'll! I am still around! – And I have a message for those yellow – bellies – sick minded_____!!

(message)_ _ You didn't get the job done! – You miss your mark not killing me! – what, you white boys didn't realized! – Is, you'll have resurrect an ongoing urge to fight! – and you can tell Jim Crows, to go to hell!!_ _ _.

After speaking for twenty five minutes Mrs Joyners end saying: "_ _ _Next, I would like to thanks the local chapter of the N. A. A. C. P. – and my employers here at the radio station. – For thinking enough of me! – in honoring me, the woman of the year award.

_ _ _So in conclusion, I am asking every able bodies black person – standing here today! – To go out, into each of down town Greensboro restaurants! – sit down at theirs lunch counters! – and demand, to be serve! _ _ _

_____ Say – Say and her group were among the first to reach Woolworth. At the lunch counter Say –Say ask the waitress: "_ _ _May I have a menu please?". Say – Say ask.

This waitress look across the counter and shouted: "_ _ _ Nigger gal! can't you read!". – Pointing to the sign on the wall which read: 'niggers and dogs are not allowed'.

Say – Say face change color; after reading the sign. Reaching across the counter Say – Say grabbed the apron string of this waitress. Pulling her partially over the counter Say – Say snap, saying:

"_ _ _Huhhh, niggers and dogs are not allowed huhhh!". Now fingering for this waitdress neck.

This waitdress yelled: "_ _ _Nigger gal! Turn me – ar – Loose!'" she yelled.

Her loud outcry, brought two other white customers to come to her aid. Just minutes before severals uniformed cops rush in with their guns draw.

The first cop yelled: "_ _ _all you niggers are under – arrest! – Don't no–body move!!".

Littler Tony was sitting at the counter. In his owns littler world. Puffing onto his long black pipe. Just then, the other cop shouted: "_ _ _Hey boy! Turn your blk ass around; and put your hands into the air!".

Tony swirl around on his stool while snatching his pipe from his mouth. Suddenly, one single shot was firer! Hitting Tony in the forehead_ _ _He was dead before his body hit the floor. A pool of blood rushs from his head. Say –Say screamed: " _ _ _ ar shit! – You just kill my cousin!!". While the other cop shouted "_ _ _that boy was reaching for his gun!". Say – Say shouted – back: "_ _ _that was his pipe! – You Jackass – ". Now advancing aggressively toward this cop.

I jump in between Say – Say and this cop and shouted: "_ _ _Please Say – Say – Don't give this S.O.B. another reason to shoot you too!", I shouted.

Smiling that same cop whisper: "_ _ _you better listen to him gurle!". His gun now pointed. "Because my triggers fingers; Is itching to shoot another one of you people!". He snap.

Say – Say fell to the floor crying: "_ _ _ This shit ass just kill littler Tony!", she cry – out.

_____ News of the shooting travel fast. Within minutes that restaurant was flooded with investigators. As they carry littler Tony Joyners body out: Hundreds of Negros demonstrators lined the side – walks –saying: "_ _ _ Black – lifes – matters – black – lifes matter – blk lifes_ _ _".

Once again, tragedy striked this Joyner's families. First with Say – Say brother. Then her father John Henry then Sadie. Then the bruter shooting of Mrs Joyners and now littler Tony! When will it all end!

The killing of Tony Joyners gain national attention. Even tho the President made a negative opinion! When he tweeted:"_ _ _I don't have nothing against negros! – But when Mr Joyners was told to turn around and put his hands up! – He should have done so_ _ _'.

_____ Tony Joyners was given a public funeral at Greensboro City Park. His 76 years old grandmother pre form the eulogy from her wheel chair in front of a pulpit. Trembling, she said: "_ _ _ Lord it's hard living life! If you're black like me! – It's hard just living! – If the value of your life is deem indispensable!

(Pause)_ _ _It's like walking through a tunnel of prejudices! Surrounded by a host of adversary's – where each step you take; could very well be your last!

_ _ _ Let us pray! – God of the universe! – Father of this world! Grant us peace on this path- way of understanding! – Grant us, oh Lord! – Righteousness on this road of Justice! – and steadfastness in ours time of change! – Transform ours hearts to love ours enemies! – Even tho, they love us not! – All these things we ask in Jesus name we pray_ _ _Amen

_ _ _ Black – Lifes matter! In this land that decree and declare! – That all men are created equal! – These words were written by our fork – tonques – white brothers. Which alleged we hold these truths to be self evidence _ _ _

Black – Lifes – Matters! – Even when, red – necks white men – dress themselves up in police uniforms! Authorize themselves empowering Jim – Crows – Going out, taking the lives of black men!

_ _ _Black – Lifes – Matter! Even in the United–States! – when a segregate – majesty of whites! – still believe under – handedly! – that white is suprarenal!

_____ Mrs Joyners took a brief pause. While wipping tears away. She continue: " _ _ _In this country, statistics have shown that it is much easy for a black man, to be gunned down in the streets of America! – Then to be killed by a heart – attack! – Blacks – Lifes – Matters _ _ _!

There wasn't a set of dried eyes in city park that day when Mrs Joyners finish speaking. Hundreds of mourners, some from both races! – And many were from as far away.

Note to the reviewer. This entire story is written in Gullah – slang language! Do not alter or replace any words or phase!

As Washington D.C. The death of Tony Joyners could have been the mid way point. Within ours civil right struggle. During this eventful – period. Few words could describe the hurt of Colored People: (the song)

_ _ _Just like the river! I've been running ever since! – It have been a long time – com – ing! – But I know! – ar – change gona come!

– CHAPTER FIVE –

_____After littler Tony death. Say – Say moved out from her mother. And start shackle- up with Tim. Although she had dropped out of school. Tim persuaded her to attend adult school. Where she eventually got her G. E. D.

After Say – Say got her G. E. D. she went to a two year college. Getting a journalism's degree. Today, Say –Say and her husband; now congress – man Timothy Johnson were celebrating another mile stone. Where Say – Say had completed 2 years in school-ing.

Fast forward. Say – Say had excel academically, at the top of her class. Today, Say –Say was deliving a valed – Victorian's address. Before her graduating class.

_ _ _Good Evening! – Today, I would like to title my address – The struggle – of black people! – In theirs quest for civil rights! – (she pause) _ _ _Every since we were brought here! – colored – people have been on a up hill battle for equality!

_ _ _For more then 100 years now. – colored – people have protest – picket – demonstrated ours disapproval – of – Jim Crows Laws! – Thousands have martyrdom their lifes – for the cause of freedom – and just in case some of you'll – may have miss my title! – I am talking about the struggle of blk. people; In theirs quest for civil right!!

_ _ _ For more then 125 years now. – colored people have been seeking those rights! – most whites take for granted! Equal – educational – opportunities – Equal employment opportunities – Equal housing – Equal –Political rights! – (she paus agan) the struggle for black people; In theirs quest for civil rights _ _ _

Her speech continue for 45 minutes. Her power of concerns, express and reveal her authentic – belief for her people and I belive this speech marks her destined. For her life.

_____ That evening after graduation. Say – Say and Timothy concur back at theirs home. Timothy was first to speak: "_ _ _Mrs Johnson, how you made it through to get your diploma; Is beyond me!" Timothy whisper.

Smiling, Say – Say Reply: "_ _ _Mr. Johnson – sir! – If it wasn't for you supporting me; In having phone sex! – I don't think I would have made it _ _ _ " Say – Say laughs.

Timothy then whisper: "_ _ _ Mrs Johnson! You're still a piece – of – work!". Timothy whisper.

Say – Say respond: "_ _ _But, you've got to love it!" she reply.

Timothy said:"_ _ _Say – Say, I am crazy in love with you! – But for now we keep ours conversation free from sex!"

Say – Say then whisper: " _ _ _Ahh – Ahh, Congressman! – cain't handle this young wife??". She ask. Before answering, Tim stood and whisper: "_ _ _ Mrs Johnson! – could we table this talk until I come back from my committee – meeting_ _ _". He exit.

_____ Miles away, at our nation capitol. A secret strategy meeting; of home land security was in progress. There, this un-identify committee chairman was presiding: "_ _ _ Mr chairman sir! – since our ancestors brought all these black people into our country! – They have grown many and mightiers then us!

_ _My proposal sir! – Is we strategized a piece of legislature. That could weaken theirs strong hold _ _ _"This senetors propose_ _ _

This chairman countered saying: "_ _ _I like your ideal senator! – what if we could put together a series – of – laws! – That would attack the over all structure of black youths! – _ _ _".

_____The result of that meeting; establish the department of social services, (the D.S.S.) Their primary objective were to attack and water down. The effectiveness of discipline among black youths!

It wasn't long, before D.S.S. began imposing the child – bills – of rights such rights as:

(A)_ The right that a child can divorce their parents.

(B)_ The right that parents can no longer discipline their children.

These laws had a pro-found effect on black youths! – Especially in homes where black female were head of house – hold.

_____It was then, I saw two young negro – males – walking down the street. Theirs pants were hunged below their waist. And every other word they spoked were blaspheme_ _ _ "Mother____ this and mother_____ that!" _ _ _

And I saw with my own's eyes! One blk mother, being arrested! And put into the rear of a paddy- wagon. All because she was caught chastising her son! In public.

And I heard this black woman yelled from that paddy – wagon: "_ _ _Lord! – What's this world coming to! – I cain't beat my owns child! – When he do's wrong!_ _ _"

It was then, another blk woman; standing on the side walks, nearby say: "_ _ _I feel you gal! – I won't raised nothing, I cain't beat! – And I damned won't feed them!". This woman shouted_ _ _

Still another woman standing near shouted: "_ _ _ we're being attack by Jim – Crows!_ _ _".

_____While witnessing all these eradicate behavor's; of young blacks. And seeing how, the white man recreation drugs. Had capture many blacks. Sending them back into slavery! Say – Say voiced: "_ _ _And this is volunteer – slavery it's a damn shame! – All these young blacks would one day. Become ours future!", Say – Say whisper.

Johnson reply: "_ _ _I am affraid so, and many of those boys. Were raised in homes without fathers figure! – They don't know what it's like to be a man!"_ _ _

Say – Say whisper: "_ _ _That's sick, to say the lease!". _ _ _

Johnson end – saying: "_ _ _ can you imagine what ours future world would be like; with them in charges!"_ _ _

_____Say – Say was selected to replace her grand – mother. At the radio station. As a talk show host. Following the foot steps as a civil right activate she had proven, she could fit the big shoe! By being a forced to be reckon – with!_ _ _

Today, in one of her commentary. She broadcast the following!

"_ _ _Good Evening, my name is Sarah Johnson! – Today, I will talk about. What it is like embodied as a black person! – In this world dominated by whites!!

_ _ _Freedom appeared to be shelter – by a race of sick minded! – strong headed white group of people! – Whom heads are filled with hatred and prejudices! – If asked, 'what's it like to live in this world as a black person?? (pause)_ _ _ Hell, it's like a living night –mare!_

_ _What – it's like to live in this world as a blk person!! – Its like breathing, in – haling and exhaling one tragedy after another, daily! – embodied with the need of human rights! – All wrapped up! – in civil rights!

_ _ _That, is what is like – living_ _ _

_____Sarah Johnson talk show had gain notoriety; In denouncing segregation. Her mounding insults were increasingly stirring up numeous threats against her life.

White folks were coming out of the wood –works; making all kind of threats! Today, Sarah had been invited to speak at a town hall meeting

At this back wood littler country town. Just ten miles north of Greensboro. She had been a littler susceptible, in accepting this invitation so far out in the boom – dock!

But, against her better judgement, she had agree! When she drove her littler Toyota across the rail road track into town. Time – nostalgia, seem to go back 50 years!

When she shift her gear stick into park just in front of this frontier looking building. She notice, while getting out. Severals suspicious looking whites men; stirring at her.

So, she hurriedly rushs through the door that was marks with the printed letters, Moses – Barber – Shop.

Once inside, she was greeted by a bunch of faces of people who look like her: " _ _ _ Mrs Johnson! Glad you could make it; we've been waiting!". This voice belong to Mr Moses the barbers.

_____She was then ushered before a littler make shift podium. Where she began speaking: " _ _ _Good evening folks! My name is Sarah Johnson – from the black suggestive – talk – show! (pause) since re – construction, this white race had been on the come – back – trail! To re-capture his superiority!

_ _ _You see, she lower her voice "_ _ _ when all those whites men came back from the civil war! They found themselves short in governing control! You see, mister Lincoln had issue a constitution amendment. Free-ing all blacks men! Giving them a seat at the table of governs! With the power – to vote!

_ _ _These whites men knew – If they re – take control! They first had to stop all black – folks! – at the polls, from voting! – Jim Crows tactices began terrorizing black folks with a vengeance! – It wasn't long before these red – necks white boys! – Had re –taken control!–_ _ _

Mrs Johnson spoke for 30 minutes before ending: "_ _ _My – brothers and my sisters! – what ever you'll do! Please don't sit around here and let these rednecks. Piss all over you'll; and tell you'll it's rain-ing_ _".

_____ Mrs Johnson rushs away from that town meeting without getting a thank you. From the group leaders. Speeding, while crossing over the rail –road track. She notice from her rear – view mirror. That she was being follow. Apparently, by those same suspicious looking white men. She saw just before entering that town hall meeting. Her fear escalate, when this vehicle rear – ended her with such devasted – impact! It causes her to jammed her accelerators! Causing her car to speed – up! Extremely fast_ _ _

_____ Mrs Johnson knew, these whites men; were out for blood! Though she wasn't ready to become their sacrificer lamb!

She mumble: "_ _ _Ain't no way, I am gona stop back here; on this country road". After driving near 8 miles. She exit onto the main high way. At the second traffic – light. She was pulled over by two whites cops.

Who hurriedly rushs – up along side her car . The first cop yelled. " _ _ _Gal!! – What's your hurry? – Let me see your drivers license and proff of insurance _ _ _" 1st cop whisper.

Mrs Johnson snap – saying: "_ _ _officers! – There's a car chasing me!", she tried to explain.

_____After the 1st cop examine both I.D. He walk back facing Mrs Johnson and shouted:

"_ _ _Mrs – Sarah – got damned – Johnson! – are you that talk show host woman?? – who has been causing us – whites – folkes! – So much troubles?", he asked.

Mrs Johnson frowned and reply: "_ _ _That would be me officer's! – In living color!", she whisper.

This first cop then snap –saying: "_ _ _well – kiss my grit!!", 1st cop yelled.

_____Moving forward, attempting to put cuffs on her. This second cop shouted: "_ _ _ Gal! we got to take you down – town – for farther question – nings!".

Mrs Johnson rebel, snatched her hands away! This 2nd cop shouted – agan: "_ _ _look woman!! – Don't make me, have to shoot yout black – ass!". While gripping a hand full of her hair.

The arrest of Sarah Johnson was highly esteem for these two rookies – cops. It was like, they had just won the lottery! calling their precinct head – quarter giving the news, they had just arrested Sarah – Johnson! Thee – agitators! – whites folks most trouble – some adversary. "_ _ _captain sir! Let it be known! We're bringing in this wench! –Sarah Johnson all hog – tie – 10 – 4!_ _ _

_____Arriving at head – quarter, they were greeted; by a long line of fellow officers. All applauding, clapping showing their approvler!

Mrs Johnson face appear as if, she had been in a fist –fight! As they escorted her inside before formally booking her; They farther interrogated her. Where, for the first time. Mrs Johnson was lost for words.

Twenty four hours later. Mrs Johnson was brought before a judge. And given a celebratory – hearing. The court room was fill with news reporter's. There, she had her husband congressman Johnson to represent her.

_____In the courtroom Mr. Johnson cited: "_ _ _your honor – sir! – If it pleases the court! I will represent my wife, Mrs Johnson!".

This judge shouted: "_ _ _I will allowed that boy! – Go ahead you've the floor!".

Congressman Johnson then said: "_ _ _ Your – honor – sir! – would you look at Mrs Johnson face! Any – one could clearly see!_ (he pointed)_ _ _she had been baten.

Just then, this judge interrupted and say: "_ _ _Mr Johnson sir! – Did you not read in the Police Report what my two officer said about your wife injury! That she just trip and fell on her face while getting into theirs squad car! _ _ _ ".

Congressman completely lost it. He shouted: " _ _ _They're telling a got – damned lie!! – she couldn't have goten those kind of wounds just – tripping over _ _ _"

This judge shouted: "_ _ _watch it boy! Mind your mouth in my courtroom before I charge you with contempt!! _ _ _

_____ Say – Say spoked for the first time. Now standing, she shouted: " _ _ _your honor! – These two pigs! Rough me up, pretty bad! – All because my name is Sarah Johnson!". She shouted.

This judge end saying: "_ _ _Like I said before woman! I am releasing you on a $500 bond! – Pay the clerk and you're free to go_ _ _".

_____Mrs Johnson appeal the judge decision. Citing that not only was she beaten! But her first amendment right was violated.

She claim: _ _ _freedom of speech – falsely arrested and slanding her name_ _

Congressman Johnson lised his prestiges. And appeal his wife case. All the way to the 5th circuit court. Un-fortunately, the case was thrown out! In the judge words: "_ _ _There's not enough credible evidence! _ I am not gona waste anymore tax payers – monies – this case is dismiss_ _ _!".

_____Colored People the story continue. In summary from the emancipation – republicanism. To the new deal democracy's. This new reformed government change its course in history and selected a black man for president. His name, Barack – Obama.

Although most historians wouldn't tell you Mr. Obama came into office; Through the backdoor for he , (Mr. Obama) had not been around the political arena long! He was virtually unknown_ _ _In other words, Mister Obama caught this white government, blind sided!

_____After C.N.N. News reported that a colored man had won the presidency. Negros all across the United States celebrated. In Chicago, some Negros were seen crying with tears of joys; In the streets!

One television station broadcast an interview; of a segregationers: "_ _ _watch my words! That Obama boy! Will be assassinated just like that nigger – loving, kennedy boy!

The election of Mister Obama came as a light at the end of the tunnel. For ours struggle. Many Negros were beginning to feel better. About theirs chances, of attaining theirs civil rights! And, about themselves. _ _ _ The words of the song, said it, all so well! _ _ _ say it loud! – I am black and I am proud_ _ _Mr James Brown.

_____While Negros were still celebrating. President Obama went live, on prime time net – work. To address the nation: "_ _ _Good Evening my fellow Americans! – I want to make it unmistakable clear! – I wasn't elected as your democratic president – nor as your Republican president! – I Barak Obama will represent all the people! – of this great nation!- _ _ _ And I have vowel to protect and defend the constitutional – rights – for all men! I will re – emphasis – that blacks – lifes – matter! – I will _ _ _

That initial speech, climax mister Obama honey moon, as being president!

Ten days later, Mr. Obama went before congress and propose a health care program. This project, immediately put his presidency's behind the 8th ball!

And for the following four years. Mr Obama found himself defending his rights; Just to be president! He was in a hot – bed with racism's – extreism's!

_____Say – Say was in her early thirties. Until now, she had a pretty successful life. Though she was still bewitched with Nymphomania. She has a good marriage to a good man and 3 lovely kids! Still all of this wasn't enough to nullify her excessive desire for sex!

To make matters worst. Today, she was hit by a scandel of having an outside affair. This scandel had turn Say –Say world up –side – down!

The people at the radio station. Were threaten to force – closure on her contract. And her mothers had call, chastising her! Yet, in spike – of it all; Timothy stood by her side.

Meanwhile, Say – Say confront Tim: "_ _ _ Tim honey! I am most appreciate! – That you stood by me! – In spike – of what that whistle – blowers said_ _"

Tim reply: "_ _ _Say – Say! – As long as you didn't go behind my back with that man!", Tim whisper.

Say – Say snap – saying: "_ _ _Tim, as horny as I gets sometimes; I wouldn't think of being with another man!", Say – Say whisper.

_____After walking away. Say – Say had a self – conscious – awaking. She had not been completely honest with Tim. She was hoping that this whole thing would blow – over!

Though she couldn't stop thinking who was behind such malicious and defamatory scandal! Then it all came back to her._ _ _ The rumor out on the streets! Said: _ _ _That the klans had put out. 'Code – names – Jim Crows! Against every member of this Joyners families. These whites – boys were out for vengeance!

_____Segregation cuts deep among and against the Negro Race Black People had to content with a financial practice. By banks credit – union; and other lending agency.

Many of these establishments practice a predatory – interest – plot! That preyed specifically on blacks! And, to top things off!–All of these lending institutions. Were pre – advise by three of the largest groups of credit score bureau. Each imposing a dictatorial version of Jim Crows Laws. Regardless what your credit score; If you're black your chances of getting the loan were slim to none!

_____Locally, many whites had left the running of city government to blacks. Eighty- five per-cent of big namesz businesses were now franchise out to blacks.

In fact, on this Tuesday election day. Blacks were running for every office from city councilmen to mayor! But, the race that was creating so much controversial (the mayor race) were most disputable!

In the mayor race, a high school principal, (Mr. Good fellow) was running against a white female encumbrance, (Mrs Mae Bell Wandermaker's). Already a two term mayors.

Mrs Wandermaker's was marry to a black man; and was the mother of three molases kids. Strangely, mayor Wander –maker's was running on a champagne – Slogan: '_ _ _Blacks – Lifes – Matter'

However, in a computer poll, taken by the Greensboro news. Mayors Wander-maker's had a two – to – one margin

Un-fortunately, on the last day; before the election. Greensboro local news channel; Dropped a bomb – shell announcement. Appealingly, mayor Wander-maker's father. Who was the founder and the acting President; of the confederate – sons of America! Had contribute 50% of the financing. Toward his daughters champaque.

In an interview, Mrs Wander-maker's was quoted: "_ _ _It's no secret that my fathers; Is the founder's of the confederate sons organization! (she pause) Yes, its true my fathers contribute a large portion of monies to my champagne!" Mayor Wandermakers citied.

This reporter then ask: " _ _ _ Mayor's Wandermakers! – you're running your platform on the slogan! – That blacks – lifes – matter! – when your father is president of a hate group – that defy everything about – black – lifes!" This reporter voiced.

Mayor Wandermaker's snap – back , shouting: "_ _ _Mr reporter – sir! My father don't have a prejudice bone in his body! – His only concern is that black folks stay in their lane! – Having said that, I want you and the voters to know. I am the proud mother of three molases – kids! _ _ _". Mayor's angerly shouted.

_____After that interview, Mayors Wander-maker's won by a land – slide. She went on and became the longest lasting mayor's; In Greensboro history!

There's an old saying. When it rain, its pour! – Today, Say – Say had a second man to come foreward and made an acquisition saying he too, had an affair. With Congressman Johnson wife.

This was a designated blow for Say – Say. When Tim confronted her. She snap – saying: "_ _ _Tim! – of all the people in this world! – You should know, how strong my desire for sex have been!", she whisper.

Tim ask again: " _ _ _Sarah! Did you have an affair with that man??", Tim ask.

Say – Say puzzierly answered: "_ _ _Tim! – It wasn't no big deal! – I hooked – up with that man, one time! – And that was out of a heated passions – of need!", she whisper.

Tim angerly reply: "_ _ _Need – my – ass!", Tim shouted. Now speeding, out the room.

Timothy later filed for a divorce. Although he continue living under the same roof with Say – Say. He moved over into the bachelor's suite. At the other end of their town house.

_____The following eight months. Tim spend some sixteen hours a day at work. Anything! Just to get away from what his wife; had done to him!

Of course, there were more than enough excitement on the job, to keep him busy! Today, over in front of city hall. A group of white citizens were demonstratings over a city – ordinance.

Giving blacks the rights to become residents; of this city high – rise apartment building. Up until now, this group of whites residents had by pass the federal statue on housing. And had maintain their lily – white exclusion. Today they protest: "_ _ _ two – four – six – eight!! – we don't want to in – tergate!–two – four – six – eight!! – we don't want to in – ter – gate!!!". Some two dozens whites sang. While marching in front of city hall.

_____This dispute came about over a grand – father – clause extending back from Jim Crows era.

It was frustrating to say the lease. Here we have a situation where blacks were in a majority. But because of this grand – fathers – clause; It disenfranchise blacks from moving in_ _ _a segregated mess!

Meanwhile over on the other side of town. In this white cemetary. Severals whites were standing in protest blocking the entrance – way. As this black funeral procession attempt to enter. The burial ground this angry white mobs start shouting racial insults: " _ _ _

ours parents would turn over in their graves! – If we allowed that nigger body! To be bury here!". They shouted.

_____Even in death, whites wasn't ready. To accept blacks. Lying – dead next to them _ _ _.

It had been one full year since Say – Say and Tim separate. This evening Say – Say swallow her pride and confront Tim. Nervously, she took that long walk down the hallway. To the other side of their five bedroom condominums. As she walk through the door. She shouted: "_ _ _ Timothy! You – got a minutes?", she ask.

Timothy snap – saying: "_ _ _Say – Say, what do you want now?". He ask

Say – Say plead: "_ _ _Tim! I had to swallow my pride; and come over here to tell you! I am sorry! I know I've been un – faithful! But if you could fine it in your heart, to forgive me _ _ _!" she beg kneeling now. She continue "_ _ _Tim!! I have been a murders, an adulterous! Even an excessive pig for sex! But never once have I stop loving you! Please will you forgive me??"

Timothy intervene and say: "_ _ _ stop Say – Say! – Is this that part of shakespears play; where Macbeths beg for mercy??", Timothy ask.

Say – Say snap – saying: "_ _ _Damned right, I ain't too proud to beg! – I want my husband back _ _ _!" she whispered.

Timothy then whisper: "_ _ _Say – Say, get – up off your knees! (he pause) I forgive you!!", Timothy whisper.

_____After patching things up! Say – Say and Tim. Had a meeting in Say – Say bedroom. Nursing that long – await urge!

Three days later Say – Say went back to work. At the radio station, And continue, her attack against all of the brutal killings! Of black men by white policemen!

_____Up until now, undercover klans – policemen. Had been secretly killings black men; at an alarming rate!

Today, on Mrs Johnson first program. She made the following, opening statement: "_ _ _ warning – warning! There's a scatter battalion of red neck white men! – who was last seen wearing police uniforms! _ Rampaging through –out the united states!

Their mission, 'the destruction of blk people! Any means possible _ _ _.'

Colored People the story continue. The local chapter for the advancement of colored people (N.A.A.C.P.) announced today, that they were scheduling a blk. tie dinner to honor the grand daughters of theirs hall – of famer, civil rights warriors, Mrs Joyners.

Mrs Johnson was caught off – guard; when she found out about the honor – ing ceremony. She was thrown a bigger – loop! When she learned, she would be the k – note speaker's.

_____That evening, while Mrs Johnson was delivering her speech. She notice a strange looking U.P.S. messenger's. Pushing his way through the crowded – table arrangement. Up to the podium. Where he, politely gaved her an anonymous looking telegram

Abruptly, she stop speaking; and began – fumbling with opening the letter. (which read): "_ _ _Sarah Johnson! – Don't sleep too sound tonite! – we're coming to kill you!_ _ _".

_____After reading the telegram. Chill bumps ran down the back of her neck. Though she continue speaking: "_ _ _And who ever heard of a black man owning a has – sie field? Or having owner – ship of a pharmaceutical company! – That distributed such drugs as L.S.D., Marijuana and other!

She then pause and pointed. _ _ _How many of you'll; have witness seeing our littler neighborhood, flooded with drugs! Hell, around here, anyone can buy them! Its' so easy, it's like buying a loaf of bread at the local 7/11 store_ _ _And who do you think control the distribution of these drugs? – I will tell you!", she yelled. It's the drug – cos'tel from South America!

They have been smuggling that shit around here. By way of ours police headquarters; By a policeman named – Jail – house – Joe! – officers – Joe to some!".

She then lower her voice and whisper: "_ _ _This son – of – a – bitch! – is suppose to be fighting against these drug – Lord! Instead, old Joe! – Been the king – pin!"_ _ _

_____After speaking, Say – Say realized, she had just let the cat out of the bag! About the cos'tel, Now her life maybe in great danger.

When she walked down off the stage Tim who was sitting at the head table approach her and whisper: "_ _ _Say –Say! You just sign your death – warrant for yourself and your entire family!". He whispered.

Say – Say whisper: "_ _ _I hope not honey! – But this shit had to be told!", she whisper.

Just then, two plain clothes detectors approach us: "_ _ _councilman! – you and Mrs Johnson got to come with us downtown!" This first detectors whisper.

Say – Say protest: "_ _ _come with you'll for what??"" Say – Say ask.

1st detectors shouted: "_ _ _Look woman, it's for your own safety! – right now, your life isn't worst a plug nickel!".

Councilman Johnson said: "_ _ _so you're putting us under protected – custody?", Johnson ask.

Say – Say said: "_ _ _what about ours three kids back at the house?", Say – Say ask.

This first detectors reply: "_ _ _we've already taken-care of them!!".

_____Like clock – work, this cos'tels orginazation were already mobilizing theirs threat. To back up theirs claim; to kill Mrs Johnson. These two detectors were acting under order; from Jail – house – Joe.

_____Severals hours later. The Johnson home was bombed. The aftermath was so devastated. The coroner was un – able to identify the badly burned three bodies.

When the Johnson's got the news. The next morning. She and Tim. Were relieved from custody. Say – Say became so emotional upset! She had to be hospitalize; and administer a settlement drug.

From emergency out – patient, Say – Say was relieved. Where she and Tim went on and found what was left of their destroyed home. Investagaters were still at the seem. Plowing through the rubbish. Say – Say screamed: "_ _ _Lord! They didn't give me the chance; To have one last look! at my kids_ _ _".

_____The tragic, of losing all three children. Were Morer then Say – Say littler body could endure. It pushed her deeper into a static state of depression.

Meanwhile, at the funeral home. Say – Say and Tim sit. While attempting to negotiate final arrangement. She wept openly. This funeral director voiced: "_ _ _Mrs Johnson, don't quote me on this! – But the rumors out on the street say that your daughters were killed by the cos'tels!

This directors whisper. Frowning. Say – Say snap – saying: "_ _ _I figure they were! Especially after I had gotten that telegram!_But they've____with the wrong black sister this time!, ooooph_ _ _" she echo.

Smiling, this director said: "_ _ _Mrs Johnson!–That sound threat – ening!!"

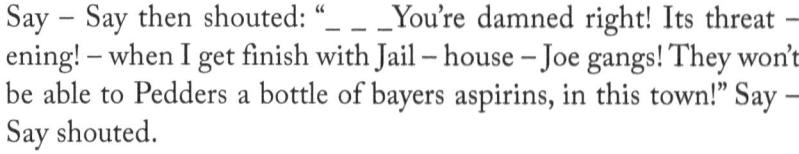

Say – Say then shouted: "_ _ _You're damned right! Its threat – ening! – when I get finish with Jail – house – Joe gangs! They won't be able to Pedders a bottle of bayers aspirins, in this town!" Say – Say shouted.

_____The Johnson's three girls funeral were one of thee largest black funeral. This city had ever had. Since her father, John Henry!

The girls funeral were held inside Greensboro high school gymnasiums where some two thousands people attended. Say – Say insist on performing the eulogy.

On the day of the funeral. Say – Say stood at this littler wooden podium. Appeared to have ice water in her veins! Her facial expression gaved the indication. This had got to be, her most difficult task yet! (she start speaking very low): "_ _ _ colored – people had been struggling in this country for hundreds – of years! – In death, some of us had to endures the mis-fortunes of being shot and killed! – or even worst, bombed! – for no other reason; then being born black!_ _ _Colored People has always been at the short end of the 'stick – of – life'. When it come to Jim – Crows – Justice! We've protest, boycott, demonstrate ours disapprovaler of how we have been treated!

_____Say – Say spoked twenty – five minutes; chopping away at racial injustice. And how Jim Crows – laws, had re – define Negros lifes! She wept openly, as she speaked. Showing her hurt!

After the death of her three daughters. Say –Say life change dramatically. She adapt a Lesbian life style. Although her relationship with Tim didn't change. They agreed on an – open – marriage.

For six months now, Say – Say lied in mourning. She couldn't believe all three daughters were taken from her; at such early age. Some days now, she was more depress then other. She prayed:

"_ _ _Father – God! – If thou would give me the strength! To get up out of my grief (pause) and give me the mindset; that I may work agan_ _ _ She prayed.

_____With all of the racial dissensions; fighting between blacks and whites. Republican's governor Margret Washington knew she had to hired two preferably blacks. To joins her staff – of – press secretary. That was when one member of her medias teams refer her to this C.E.O. of this blk Radio station; over in Greensboro. Governor Washington personally made the call. To this radio C.E.O. who gaved her Sarah Johnson name. As a perfect candidate for the job.

Up until now, Say – Say had been very reluctant about doing anything, let alone, a job! Nonetheless, after the phone call interview with the governor. Say – Say agreed on taking the Job. But only if her husband would be hired as a Lobbyist as well. After the contact sign – ing. Say – Say and Tim. Moved to the state Capitol. Where they tooked up resident inside the governor's mansion.

_____Governess Margret Washington, the state first female – white – governors. Was a undercover Lesbians! Rumors has it, that Gov. Washington conspired this deal with Say – Say; only to inspired her owns littler Lese majesty! In the governess words: '_ _ _ I need the commitment, having a piece of black pepper! – on my staff! – and a pledges to my personal needs'.

_____Timothy and Say – Say committed themselves to the governor. For two consecutive years. Gov. Washington immediately went and assign Timothy to head – up a interracial task force group.

Timothy first assignment was to hear the acquisition why two whites cops. Shouldn't be prosecuted for killing this Negro youths!

(Fast –forward) _ _ _ Apparently, members of the dead – youth family. Had filed a lawsuit against the police department for negligence! And now the public was weighting in on the dead youth side.

_____After some in – depth search of the case this task force ruled to pay, two – point five millions dollars. To the dead youths family. The problem was, the police union; Had an inadequate state – fund. To pay out such large amount.

In another case, the governors authorize another independent council to investigate, 'Police – corruptions, thoughtout the state. These type of work load. Were morer then enough, to keep Timothy busy; and away from their separate quarter. Their previous open – marriage – agreement made it all so easy. For Gov. Margret to have her way with Say – Say.

Meanwhile, at a secluded meeting room. In the rear of the mansion. Governor Margret was having an intimate experience with Say –Say. An on – going routine; that had been happening for now, two years!

_____After Say – Say and Timothy contact had expired. They return to their private life. Having no love lost between them.

Twelve months later. Timothy ran for mayors; and won by a landslide. A move, that pushed Say –Say; back out into the Job market. Where she was re-hired as a commentator's. For that same radio station. Her grand – mother had work.

It was like theirs lifes had not stop revolving around the civil rights movement. Now that Timothy had won the Mayors seat. Mostly by the strong backing from his former boss. Republicans governess Margret Washington. He had switch from the democratic to the Republicans party.

This change of party, brought on a conflict between he and Say – Say. Although Say – Say struggle to accept the Republicans! As her party – of – choice.

Today, Say – Say confront Tim: "_ _ _Tim! – Why did you switch to the Republicans Party?" Say – Say ask.

Timothy answered: "_ _ _Honey! The Republicans Party were the Party of ours ancestors – back during re – construction – period!".

Say – Say snap saying: "_ _ _ Tim! – I don't care about that! – Them Republicans have always been too uppity for me!" Say – Say whisper.

Tim then said: "_ _ _Honey, why would you say that! – Back during re – construction our ancestors were all Republicans! – And they ran the government!".

Say – Say shouted: "_ _ _ Timothy! Got – damned, you're forgetting one thing! (pause) back then, a group of Republicans – whites! Retaliate and put booths to our's black – Legislators asses!" she screamed.

Tim shook his head and reply: " _ _ _Say – Say! you got it bad! – You're eaten – up, with hatred against whites people!", Tim frowned.

Say – Say whisper: "_ _ _ Tim! Have you forgotten what those Republicans bastards did to ours three daughters! – How they brutally – bombed our home! Killing our childrens! – In the worst kind of way!", she sobbed.

Tim then whisper: "_ _ _Honey! – The bible said, we've got to forgive and forget!", Tim whisper.

Screaming now, Say – Say shouted: "_ _ _well, goody – two shoe to you Tim! – For me, I haven't gotten to that point yet _ _ _of forgiveness!", she shouted.

_____ (Retrospecting) I remember one F.B.I. investagators saying shortly before our home was bombed. Three Mexican's looking men were seen rushing from our house. They were escorting 3 small girls; Into a black S.U.V.

_ _ _Could my daughters still be alive today. She ask her self.

After that encounter, Say – Say went back to the Radio station and prepare to broastcast her mini – series. Sitting before a small microphone:

On the air: " _ _ _ Good Evening, this is the Sarah Johnson talk show! I am Sarah Johnson – And today I will be speaking on the first phase; of a mini – series! of the U.S. constitution, its pros and cons!! All of that and more, after these words from our announcements!

(Minutes later) Did you know this nation constitution were written by a group of white men? That compose and pen in theirs opening phase. (Pre – amble)_ _ _ We hold these truths, to be self – evidence – that all men are created equally!'. S – T – O – P! Now when those white boys wrote this! They wasn't talking about colored – folkes! Because, at the time. There was another white boy. Down in south Carolina – who had just mandate a Law – declaring colored folkes; as being only 4/5 human!

(She continue) _ _ _ Among these are life, liberty and the pursue of happiness! S – T – O – P!! agan these white boys didn't give – a – shit! About our happiness! At the time, all of them owns hundreds of slaves; and the only pursue of happiness they care about were. That we work theirs fields – and look the other way. While they pleasure ours women!

_ _ _ To secure these rights, government is instituted among men. Deriving their just powers from the consent of the governments! STOP! This government have proven its unable to secure civil rights! For coloreds – even tho. Their constitution say – so!

_ _ _All of these rights – could best been written on a roll of toilet paper! – Because when it come to black americans! – All theirs rights have been violated. – Their young men gunned down and killed! – Theirs women folks rape! – Theirs lifes mock by a kangaroo court, Judge by Jim Crows _ _ _ I am your host! – Sarah Johnson _ _ _

_____ When Sarah walked out of that broad – cast room. She was approach by another U.P.S. delivery man: "_ _ _Mrs Johnson! – I have a telegram for you!", He whisper now while he passed the telegram to her.

Frowning Sarah reply: " _ _ _ Yes, I am Mrs Johnson; I'll take that!".

About that time, Tim walk – up and said: "_ _ _Another telegram Sarah?". Tim ask_ _ _

While opening the letter. Sarah mumble: "_ _ _ Yes, I wonder who it's from this time!" Sarah whisper.

Tim inquisitively ask agan: " _ _ _well Sarah, who is it from?", Tim ask.

Sarah mumble dumb – founded: " _ _ _ I don't know, all it say is: 'Mrs Johnson! We've another bullet out, with your name on it!" Sarah whisper.

Tim then yelled: "_ _ _ I knew it. I knew it! Sarah, you got to stop criticizing those people! – You see what it did to ours daughters!!". Tim shouted

Sarah whisper: " _ _ _Tim, as much as I want to stop! – I just cain't, the true shit need to be told!". Sarah declared.

Shaking his head in disbelief: Tim whisper: "_ _ _ Its your funeral, but them buck – er –ler's not gona continue let you redicule them, on your talk show!".

Sarah profoundly whisper: " _ _ _If they kill me Tim! – My eyes have seen the glory of the com – ing of freedom!

Changing subject: she said: " _ _ _Tim – honey, will you take me home; and make sweet love to me_ _ _". She ask.

_____ Twenty minutes later, Say – Say sit facing Tim on top of a king size bed. Completely nude, with a chess board in their mid. Timothy broke silent – saying:

"_ _ _Mrs Johnson! It have been a minute since we made love. I thought you would never ask!" Tim whisper.

Smiling Say – Say pointed – saying: "_ _ _White man move first!". She whisper while folding her arms around her naked upper body.

Tim then said: "_ _ _ Honey! I move my white pawns to your black – kings – pawns – 4! Tim whisper.

Say – Say shooked her head and said: "_ _ _ Oh No! I am gona move my black – pawn to your Queen – bishop – pawn – 3!

Tim said: "_ _ _ I counter my white pawn to your black – Queen pawn – 4!", Tim whisper.

Say – Say snap – saying: "_ _ _ Really Tim! I counter my black – ass pawn – Queen to the fourth position!", Say – Say whisper.

_____ After making his thirteen moves, Timothy boasted: "_ _ _ Say – Say! There ain't nothing in the rules book; that Say, I cain't have two or more Queens at one time!", Timothy boasted.

Frowning, Say – Say warned: "_ _ _ watch – it sucker! – Beside, if I move my ass right; I can seduce two of your rooks and bishops!", she warned. then add. "_ _ _Because this black sister ain't gona let you have that kind of Queenings – potentialities!

Tim then said: "_ _ _Time out, time out! – what are we playing, chess or botty – call??", Tim ask.

Say – Say then said: "_ _ _Tim, I cain't speak for you; But I am playing touch – and move!", Say – Say whisper.

Tim then laughs and say: "_ _ _ Oh littler lady, I am about to castle my king on the Queen side!", Tim boast.

_____And then it was all over. The next day, the Greensboro time. Printed an article where a genealogist studies. Found a trace, linking a small black family. Living right here in Greensboro. To one of the founding fathers – presidents! It was the talk of the town.

That same day, Mayor's Johnson appointed his wife, (Mrs Johnson). To head – up a task – force group to investigate that un – solve mystery – killings! About those 3 black girls!

This appointment was right down Say – Say alley. Up until, after 12 months. There had been no leads or arrest.

Upon inquiry, Say – Say went back to the original – police report. And came across a smoking gun – piece of new evidence! The report said, 'Shortly before the explosion. Three men were seen running from the house. Shortly before the explosion. But no where in the report; Say anything about these 3 men being question.

Say – Say was like a blood hound. Once she come up on a scent – of evident. _ _ _ She charge full speed ahead! She first send an e – mail; to solicitor's Tom Gamble. From her husband office computer. And she address the memo, urgent!

_____ Investigators – solicitor's Gamble sign – off on the incident – report. And its he, who have the authority to re – open the case.

When Say – Say came into Timothy office she confronted him on her finding:

"_ _ _ Honey! – I found a smoking – gun piece of evident; I believe could nail them sons – of – a bitches! – who killed ours girls!" Say – Say whisper.

Mayor's Tim voiced: "_ _ _ Say – Say, you don't have the authority nor the power; to go after those men!" Mayor's whisper.

Say – Say countered: "_ _ _Mister – Mayors – sir! – You appointed me to head – up this investagation! That gaved me the legal – power,

To go after theses sons – of – a – bitches!! (pause) That's why I summon solicitors Gamble to come, to your office!

Mayors shouted: "_ _ _you – what??", while solicitor's Gamble enter the office, unannounced.

Gamble immediately ask: "_ _ _Mr. Mayors – sir! – Did you summon for me to come over?".

Say – Say intervene and said: "_ _ _ The Mayor didn't but I did!", Say – Say snap saying.

Surprise, Gamble voiced: "_ _ _ oh – good evening Mrs Johnson! – what can I do for you?", Gamble ask

Mayors Tim intervene and say: "_ _ _Mr. Gamble, would you closed the door and have a seat!", Mayor's Tim whisper.

_____ While Gamble closed the door. Mayors Tim whispered: "_ _ _My wife here seem to think; she have dug – up evident! – on that house – bombing – killing – case! That you should re – open the case! Mayors whisper.

Say –Say interrupte – saying: "_ _ _Mr. Gamble! If you had taken your head, out from under officers Joe behind! – You would have found this_____! Say – Say – snap – saying.

Gamble snap and ask: "_ _ _ Found what!", Gamble ask _ _ _

Say – Say voiced: "_ _ _Right here in the police report, 'that 3 men were seen running away from the house _ _ _!

Gamble said: "_ _ _ oh, these 3 men were members of the bomb – squad! – who were call, to de – activate the bomb _ _ _!".

Say – Say snap agan and said: "_ _ _ Mr. Gamble! You mean to tell me; these 3 men were to call to de – activate the bomb! – before the explosion! – and what was each of these three men carry – ing; away from the house?_", she ask.

Frustrated, Gamble snap – saying: "_ _ I – don't know Mrs Johnson! – They could have been taking theirs equipment back to theirs truck _ _ _

Say – Say shouted: "_ _ _ Tom Gamble!! – Do I look like I've s – t – u – p – i – d! written on my fore head!" (pause)_ _man, don't pussy – foot with my intelligence!".

Gamble rose to his feet, snap – and said: "_ _ _come on Mrs Johnson! Do you expect me to re – open this case; on that evident alone?", Gamble ask.

Mayor Tim interrupt: "_ _ _Mister – Gamble – sir! My wife might get a littler over emotional at times; But, on this, I believe she's right on it! – (pause) _ _ _I want you to re- open this case too! – oh Mr Gamble will you closed the door on your way out _ _ _"

Say – Say then whisper: "_ _ _ Thanks honey, on backing me up!", she whisper.

Mayor's Tim whisper: "_ _ _ No, thank you, after all, we were talking about ours – three daughters! _ _ _"

_____ Reluctantly, solicitors Gamble petition to get this case – re – open. Knowing all so well; he had to answer to his under cover – boss. (Jail house Joe). He then had the 3 men brought in for question – ing; And later books! – await-ing trial, knowing they would be represented by a group of criminal lawyers. The best, that money could buy!

It wasn't no secret everybody knew that crime – Lord, Jail – house – Joe; was calling the shots. And there was a price now, on the head for Sarah Johnson_ _ _ revenge is a bad_____!!

_____Meanwhile, severals heavely armed men attack the radio station; with a commandos – type assaults! Hitting the building on all side!

When Say – Say rushs out her broad – cast studio. One assassins bullet, ricochet off the east – wall! Hitting Say – Say in the forehead.

Causing severe damage. Five other radio employees were killed. Say – Say was lucky!

This racketeers assaults without doubt; was the brain – child of cos'tels boss, Jail – house – Joe.

_____ Say – Say was rushs to the emergency hospital. Where she underwent 5 hours of surgery. This terrorism attack came just short of taking her life.

One hour after coming out of recovery. Say – Say was being question by this investigator's.

"_ _ _Mrs Johnson! – Sorry, but I've to ask you a couple of questions! – You're like a cat with 9 lifes! – Do you have any ideal, who was trying to kill you??", This investigator's ask.

Say – Say broken voice mumble: "_ _ _ I have no doubts; It was Jail – house – Joe!!". Say – Say weakly mumble.

This investagators voice: "_ _ _Mrs Johnson! I think you already knows; that your special – council have this cos'tels – group under investagation_ _ _".

Say – Say then ask: "_ _ _Officers! – why do the cos' tels hate me so??" she ask . He smiled and say _ _ _ Mrs – J – Your talk – show have been bad – mouthing this group now, for the longest _ _ _

_____ 24 hours after the attack. Three of the assassins were arrested. And held without bond!

In as speedy trial, that lasted ten days. Acting under the supervision of a kangaroo court. After hearing the court scheduler; Say – Say secretly lefted the hospital so she could attend each day of the trial.

At the trial, she learn her three attackers were represented by attorneys. The best money could buy! While defensing these men.

Attorneys pictured these criminals – reputation! Just short of being saints!

On the seventh day of the trials. It appeared the case was headed for a mis – trail! Say – Say was devasted! As she sit there, on the back row, in the court – room. She secretly call Tim:

"_ _ _ Tim! – This hearing here is going all wrong! I think this judge might rules, a mis – trail!" she whisper through her cell – phone.

Tim whisper back: "_ _ _ Honey! In a kangaroo court! – Justice is handed out in two level! One for whites folks; and the other for us".

Say – Say whisper: "_ _ _well! If they don't convict those shit – asses! I'll do it myself! Ohh, I got to go!", (call dropped)

Tim shouted through the cell phone: "_ _ _Say – Say, Say – Say! Don't do anything fool – ish!

_____ The call dropped. When this judge loudly declare a mis – trail! Say – Say rushs foreward. Reaching, her hand in her purse. She commence firings; five rounds into one of the assassins. Before officers wrestle her to the floor. And placed her under – arrest. News break printed and reported: "_ _ _Mayors wife killed an – un – armed man in court.

__ CHAPTER SIX __

After news of the court room shooting. A computer poll was taken on weather this Negro Mayors wife would get a fair trial.

The result were un – equally divided; especially since official Joe control the polling. Twenty four hours after the public – polling. That same judge held a speedy trial for Say – Say sentencing her to five years and one millions dollars bond!:

"_ _ _Sarah – Say – Say – Johnson! I hearby sentence you, Five years and one millions dollars fined _ _ _

The song summed it up: "_ _ _The white man made the electric light – to take us out of the dark!

The white man made the cars – to take us over the road! – He then enslaved the colored man to laborious! And lift the heavy loads! – Now! He made money! To separate the rich from the poor_ _ _

_____ One million dollars was morer then Say –Say and I had accumulate in ours joint account. Although somehow, someway, I had to come up with $1,000,000 dollars to free my wife.

Shortly after the judge decision. I received an anonymous call; on my office hot line. It was the voice of a man with an accent.

"_ _ _Mister – Mayor's – sir! – we have your three daughters! – If you want to see them again alive! We want $1,000,000 dollars in small un – marks bills!".

I interrupte the caller: "_ _ _ Is this some kind of Joke! – My three daughters were all killed months ago!! ", I shouted.

The voice on the phone interrupt me saying: "_ _ _Mr Mayors! We did bombed your house! But your daughters wasn't in the house_ _ _"

I interrupte again: "_ _ _ Lier's,! Prove that my daughters are still alive!!, I shouted just before this caller said: "_ _ _ Listen for yourself!" He then put one of my girl on the phone. "_ _ Daddy – daddy please come and get us_ _ _!

Suddenly, this man voice over – shadow my daughters voice saying: "_ _ _That's enough! Mr Mayors you've just 24 hours to come up with the money! Or the next time, they will be killed for real!" (the call drop)

_____ I quickly call and reported the blk. mailer's and went and withdraw the blance of funds from the bank. While at the bank. I talk to the loan officers. About getting a loan against my Mayors salary. I was so caught – up, negotiating for this money. I completely forgot about my wife until my cell phone ring It was solicitor's Gamble calling to tell me. That they were transporting my wife to Lee county – institution for women. I ask: "_ _ _why Lee county, so far away?" Gamble whisper. _ _ _Mr Mayors! They must have assume you couldn't come up with that kind of money!! _ _ he voiced.

I weakly echo: "_ _ _They were probably right_ _ _

_____Lee county institution prison was control by the cos'tels family and crime – Lord, officers Joe! And rumor has it. Officer Joe ran the prison with an iron – fist; through two of his most trusted Lieges.

For the woman facility. Joe commission Mae – Bell – Duelee as warden. A woman who had been in prison, Most of her life.

And had been transported here from the girls reformatory _ _ _

_____ I had a sleep – less night; Anticipating, hearing from the blk. mailer's. Thought my feeling was somewhat better. Now, I had gotten the $750,000 dollars collateral loan!

With one millions dollars all in small bills. Just as the black mailers ask. My nerve were on Pins and Needle! Anticipating, hearing from the blk. mailers.

When my cell phone finally sounded. My heart skip a – beat!! "_ _ _Mister Mayors! You got the money? Here is what I want you to do.

This voice gaved a list of directions. Where to drop off the money and where, I could pick – up my girls! I didn't think about what the police said: "_ _ _To keep the caller talking long enough! – so they could trace their where- er- bout!

All I wanted, were my girls back. 20 minutes later, after dropping off the money. I found all 3 girls hands – tied, to a street sign. Marks_ school – childrens – crossing.

_____ Over – whelm with Joy! I was completely over throw! I felt I had made the right decision. In paying this $1,000,000 dollars ransom. Instead of paying the 1 millions for bond – money; for my wife. Either way, it was a hard decision!_ _ _

Human – traffick – ings hit home with me. When it came to my girls. Today, I felt like a brand new man! Life, have given me, three new reason to live! (Just thinking) Having my three girls back alive! Was overwhelming! And, I am gona treasure every – living moment!

(Alternately)_ on a sad note. My poor wife was still locked – up, in prison.

_____Meanwhile, up in Lee County – Prison. When inmate Sarah Johnson first arrived, she was separated from the other prisoners. And ushered directly over to the warden office. Upon entering this small cell like office. Warden Duelee was sitting behind her desk. With a stack of papers, in her hand. Warden immediately shouted: "_ _ _so you're Sarah Johnson! – You don't look that tuft to me! – (she pause) _ _ _I have here special orders, instructing me! – That you should be kepted in solitary confinement! – This order also states, 'to treat you rough and make you like it_ _ _".

Sarah looked and shouted: "_ _ _Yes! – I am Sarah Johnson! – To your black ass!", Sarah shouted.

Warden Duelee snap – back and said: "_ _ _Woman! – Do you know how much money you've set the cos'tel back with your mouth!

Sarah whisper: "_ _ _Not enough, and not near as much as I am gona! When I get out of this place_ _ _".

Warden DueLee voice change to a lower tone: "_ _ _ Oh sister you're gona be here; A long – ass – time!".

Her voice resemble Sadie. She then call out. "_ _ _Guards! Come put this bitch in the hole!

_____ Warden Duelee came here from the girls – reformatory. Hand pick and highly recommended by officer Joe. According to record, inmate Duelee had came a long way for a blk. woman she was now. Put in charge of running this prison system.

Acting under direct order of officer Joe Warden Duelee was now operating a prostitution ring using dozens of female inmates.

Nonetheless, today for some strange reason. After having interview this Johnson – inmate. Warden Duelee had a mindboggling incurrence. Marking a past notable event. Where she had psychological cross pass; with a girl from her reformatory – jail life.

_____Alone in her office Warden Duelee began reflexing back to the time she was incarcerated in the girls – reformatory. And how she had conspired and taken over the identity of inmate – Sadie! Whispering out loud: "_ _ _And this Johnson inmate – sister! Killed me_ _ _" She whisper before saying. "_ _ _ All is well now. I will get my revenge before she leave_ _ ".

_____Today, after weeks of investigation the F.B.I. ran a paper trail on those mark $250,000 dollars blk. mail – money. They were able to trace it back to a organization bank account. (W.M.A.D.D.) whites – mothers – against – drunk – driver's.

They later learn the C.E.O name; as being Mary Taylor. In questioning her: "_ _ _Mrs Taylor! Do you know why we brought you in?" This 1st agent ask.

Mrs Taylor answer!

"_ _ _Boys! I have no earthly ideal; unless it's that large deposit I made last week"._ _ _

The 2nd agent said: "_ _ _Mrs Taylor! You know it's because of that deposit! Where did you get such large amount of money from?".

Mrs Taylor frowned and said: " _ _ _ Boys! – I am afraid I got to take the fifth! On that question!", she whisper.

This first agent voiced: "_ _ _ pleading the fifth, Mrs Taylor! I am afraid we got to charge you with co – conspiracy to murder and black mail!"_ _ _

Mrs Taylor shouted: "_ _ _Oh hell no! – I am not going down like that! That money was donated from a fellow fraternity group! _ _ _".

The first agent ask: "_ _ _What is the name of this fellow fraternity – group?"_ _ _

Mrs Taylor reply: "_ _ _All I can tell you, is this fellow – fraternity; Is affiliated to an officer's name Joe!", she whisper.

_____After question–ing Mrs Taylor F.B.I. were able to link officers Joe to embezzlement, distribution of drugs! Human trafficking among dozens of other crimes.

Finding all these new accusation against this cos'tels – group. Solicitor's Gamble had no other choice. But to petition the court for an appeal, on Mrs Johnson case_ __.

When Mrs Johnson case was brought back before the court her charges were drop to third – degree – man slaughters. Where she was re – sentence to five years probation.

_____Mrs Johnson was release under house arrest. She had to wear a ankle bracelets; and report every 7 days, to her probation officers. Below is a paper copy, of her release:

#1_ She couldn't leave the state

2_ She couldn't have any involvement in the civil rights movement_ _

3_ She couldn't physically broadcast on her radio – show

When Say – Say first came back from prison. She spend most of her time re – union – ist with her three girls. The majority of her time. She would be in her bedroom, scripts –writing for her talk show.

Timothy enter her bedroom: "_ _ _Say – Say honey! – what are you doing now?'"Timothy ask_ _ _

Say – Say answer, not looking away from that stack of papers. On the night stand: "_ _ _I am trying to prepare my speech for my 1st episode talk show", she whisper_ _ _

Timothy shouted: "_ _ _you cain't do that! _ That's in violation to the conditions of your prorole!_ _ _

Dropping the boil – point – pen; on top of that stack of papers Say – Say snap – saying: "_ _ _ Tim honey! You haven't actually read the conditions of my re – lease! – It said, I couldn't physically broadcast my show!" Say – Say whisper.

Timothy mumble before exiting the room. "_ _ _It's your funeral!_ _"

Say –Say went back writing: "_ _ _Good – Evening, this is the Sarah Johnson talk show! – I am your host _____ standing in for Mrs Johnson – This evening ours topic will be 'colored – peoples – ours heritages! And ours language!! _ _ _ These and more – after the following from ours sponsors!

(Minutes later) about 98% of all colored – people came to the new world as slaves – coming by way of the coastal area of North Carolina – South Carolina – Georgia and Florida!

_ _ _ As slaves, they soon adopt and began speaking a dialect combination of English – based – creole and west African languages. That soon became known as Gullah!

The name Gullah evolved from the word Angola! The south – west African country where many of these enslave people originated

_ _ _On the other hand the name Geechee! – derived from the kissi – peoples of Guina – a rice loving group of people –who harvest and grew rice, starting back in Charleston south – Carolina! And, if you don't want to start a fight! Please don't call one of these people, Geechee!

_ __ That is a brief – history of colored – people – ours heritages and ours language! So until next time I am yours – tru-ly! – Standing in for Mrs Johnson _ _ _"

_____After a series of this daily radio episode. The Sarah Johnson talk show. Move up on the chart.

That was when, B.E.T. (Black – Entertainer – Television) purchase some of the rights. To broadcast; some of Sarah compositions.

This gaved Mrs Johnson, a larger audiences exposer. It also alert awareness. She was violating the term of her perole.

But, it wasn't until after she had written that smoking – gun – episode about the federal government; That cause her down fall!

Later, in this last episode Mrs Johnson wrote how the federal government was experimenting with a new weapon. That attack only people – of color! In her documentary, she wrote: "_ _ _Good – evening – This is the Sarah Johnson talk show – I am your host _____ standing in for Mrs Johnson! – This evening – I would reveal and uncover, project – top – draw'. – A government operation – where cancer – exnobiotic – agents are being deploy in ours food supplies! – All of that – plus more after the following words – from ours sponsor's!

Minutes – Later It has been disclose un – intentionally by an anonymous member of home – land – security. That ours government is conducting an under – cover operation call project – Top – Draw!!

The United States government is stock – piling and deploying an exnobitic agents – programmed to eradicate all low income people!

_____24 hours after that broadcast Mrs Johnson was arrested. This time for violating the conditions of her parole. And much like before, Say – Say was taken back to Lee County correctional institution.

Meanwhile, Mayors Johnson was beginning to experience some problems. With his 17 years old daughters. Much like her mother, she had gone out and gotten her self arrested. While picket-ing out front of the police – precinct. In retaliation for the shooting – death of a black youth who was jogging through a predominant white neighborhood.

Today, Johnson had to sit and witness – hearing. The charges read out in court: "_ _ _ All rise! – Thee honorable Jane Reid presiding!", Bailiff shouted

Judge Reid whisper: "_ _ _ You'll maybe seated! (she pause) Miss Johnson, you're being charge with parading without a permit and threat-ing to kill a police officers! – How do you plead?", Judge Reid ask

Miss Johnson stood and snap – saying: " _ _ _Well, your honor! A pig is a pig! – regardless how you cut him up! – weather in pork – chops or rump – roast _ _ miss Johnson voiced.

Judge Reid snap – saying: "_ Woman! – what are you trying to say?" Judge Reid ask_ _ _

Miss Johnson voiced agan: "_ _ _ What I am trying to say, your honor! Is black folks been struggling against these white – ass – pigs! – Too long now, just to stand by; and do nothing_ _ _".

Judge Reid interrupte: "_ _ _That's enough young lady! You made your point! – Now, I must make mine! – I fine you, six months – imprisonment! _ _ _".

_____When Judge Reid gaved her verdict It was like pouring salt, in an open wounds! – Mayor's Johnson now, had to contend with two family members in jail. Still, he had to maintain his job governing the city. And keeping his family to gather!

Upon arrival back at Lee County Prison. Say – Say again. Had a one – on – one confrontation. With warden Duelee: "_ _ _Woman! You're back here agan!-", Duelee shouted.

Say – Say snap – saying: "_ _ _Yess, I am back! – What's it to you W – O – M – A – N!"_ _ _

Warden Countered, her voice now change: "_ _ _Girl! Didn't momma tell you, there will be no nasty – stuff, in this house!_ _ _

Say- Say looked as if she had just heard the voice of a ghost. She whisper: "_ _ _ you sound just like my dead – ass sister, S – A – D – I – E!

Warden reply: "_ _ _Gal! – I am Sadie, in spirit! – You killed me once; All because of a man! – This time before you leave this prison! – I'm gona kill you _ _ _

Terrofied Say –Say whisper: " _ _ _Sadie Sadie – Mae! – you cain't be! – I kill you myself! With my bare hands!_ _ _"

_____ For some mystical way. Sadie had resurrect; into the body of Warden Duelee. Today, after witness-ing this strange encounter's; she knew she would eventually be killed _ _ _

Meanwhile, Mayor Johnson life had been continuous catastrophe after another!

Today, after hearing that his 17 years old daughter's was sentenced, to go off to jail. He sit there, in that court room, reminiscing:

_____ It wasn't too many years ago. When I first saw Say – Say! coming down that hill – side. Her face was dress, so innocently pure!

Her eyes were locked on that crowd – of demonstrators. Down near the water front. They were sing – ing: '_ _ _we – shall over – come – we shall over – come_ _ _'

And, I believe with every breathe in my body! That Say – Say, Sarah – Johnson! That day, adopt and took on the entire struggle of this civil rights movement! And put it on her shoulders! And made it, her personal struggle!

_ _ _Say – Say, Sarah Johnson! Spoked out against racial in–justice; Every chance she got! Up until the very end!

_ _ _Say – Say Sarah Johnson! fought segregation. Like a warriors, overcome with intense rage!

_ _ _Say – Say Sarah Johnson! – Is no longer with us today! She was kill, two days after returning back to prison. By her in – strange – sister Warden – Duelee!

_ _ _Say –Say Sarah Johnson! Left a legacy, challenging all black folks! To forever stand – up! Against Jim Crows! One of my wife last commentary:

"_ _ _ We shall over – come! We shall over come!! – Though they forced ours ancestors – from their home land – in Africa!

They en-slaved them – and deny them –theirs God – given – rights! – Declaring that black – folkes! Are 4/5 humans! We shall over – C – O – M – E!

_ _ _Farther, they declare in their written constitution! – That all men are created equally! – They turn around and amend another set of laws! They call Jim Crows – we still shell over – C – O – M – E!

_ _ _ When thousands of white men! Go under – cover – hiding under sheets! – Some dressed in police uniforms! With only one mission! – To exterminate black – folkes! – Any way possible! – We still shell over – C – O – M – E!

_ _ _I want to stop – right here and say to all my stiff – necks brothers! – You know who you're! ; Thee opity crew! Who feel you have attain what littler freedom all on your own! – That you pulled yourselves up by your boots straps!

Brothers! – stop fooling yourselves! – It took generation upon generations of black – folks striving togather – To get where we're t – o – d – a – y! – If we as a people! – continue, to gather, to fight segregation! – At all cost, even to the point, that each of you! – Be martyr!!

_____She then began humming the song: "_ _ _Oh – freedom, oh freedom! – Before – I be a slave! – I'll be bury in my grave!–_ _ _".

Her commentary continue: "_ _ _ I may not be there – on that great day! –When we attain ours freedom! – But, I challenge every

Negro man, woman or child! – To forever stand – and fight against segregation! _ _ _ _".

_____Colored People have always had to struggle. They have fought through some of life most difficulties challenges.

Colored People have alway been at the short end of the stick–of life. When its comes to white man Justice! Suffering through Jim Crows doctrines!

Our story Colored People! Is just one individual episode; revealing, the ignorant – characters of the white race!

After our story. Say – Say Sarah Johnson was killed during a prison up – rising.

_____ Tim, Congressman Johnson after our story, retired from public life. Became a private citizen. And live until his death.

_____ Deleah Johnson – Say – Say 17 yrs. Old daughters. After relief from prison. Got herself togather. Follow in her mothers foot – steps; and became a leading civic rights activate's.

_____ Mrs Joyner's – work with the N.A.A.C.P until her death.

_____Officers Joyners – after our story became the first Negro police chief. In a major southern city.

The End.

__ ABOUT THE AUTHOR __

F.E. Green Jr. the author was born during that era of segregation. When blacks and whites; were at war! Where the color of one's skin, dictate the atmosphere how a man life is lived!

I one quoted saying. "_ _ _I grew – up tip – toe – ing through the shadows of bigotry and prejudices! Know all too well! If I am to survive! I must learn how to stay in my place!

And hopefully, with help from Jesus – Christ! I may one day over – come! And tell the world. How I got over! And how I vow to write about some of my frustrations! Other books I have written:

A walk through the bible

Two worlds between us

Wheeler Hill – The saga

Colored People

Sermons on the mountain

To purchase a copy of these books, go to Barnes & Noble books or Amazon books _

F.E. Greene Jr.